PLANNING EDUCATIONAL VISITS FOR THE EARLY YEARS

PLANNING EDUCATIONAL VISITS FOR THE EARLY YEARS

Anna Salaman and Suzy Tutchell

Paul Chapman Publishing

The photograph on the back cover and page 25 was taken with permission from Leeds City Art Gallery

Paul Chapman Publishing
A SAGE Publications Company
1 Oliver's Yard
55 City Road
London EC1Y 1SP

SAGE Publications Inc.
2455 Teller Road
Thousand Oaks, California 91320

SAGE Publications India Pvt Ltd
B-42, Panchsheel Enclave
Post Box 4109
New Delhi 110 017

Library of Congress Control Number: 2005905290

A catalogue record for this book is available from the British Library

ISBN 1-4129-1926-6
ISBN 1-4129-1927-4 (pbk)

Typeset by Pantek Arts Ltd, Maidstone, Kent
Printed in Great Britain by Cromwell Press Ltd, Trowbridge, Wiltshire
Printed on paper from sustainable resources

CONTENTS

LIST OF IMAGES

ACKNOWLEDGEMENTS

We are very grateful for the help and information provided by the following individuals, without whom this book could not have been written.

Julie Ballinger, Frogwell Primary School; Ita Beausang; Diana Braund, Highweek Community Nursery and Primary School; Laura Broderick, Northern Architecture; Rosie Burt, Royal College of Music; Alison Chaplin, Arts On The Move; colleagues at ABL Cultural Consulting; Karen Collins, Cruddas Park Early Years Centre; Feyza Deveci, Sally Goldsworthy, and Francesca Seguiti, Discover; Gabrielle Ellis, William Davis Primary School; Chris Elwell and Paula Manning, Half Moon Young People's Theatre; Adriene Figueroa, Belfast Zoo; David Fittell, Museum Magnet Schools; Angie Groombridge, St Werburghs Park Nursery School; Joy Hamilton, Sandbrook Nursery School; Jean Harvest, Chippenham Museum; Nikki-Kate Heyes and Jill O'Sullivan, soundLINCS, Lincolnshire Music Development Agency; Chris Holmes, Sightlines Initiative; Pat Holliday, Our Lady and St Anne's Roman Catholic Primary School; Susan Hornby and Diane Porter, The Deep; Colin Hynson and Colly Mudie, Norfolk Museums Service; Meabh Ivers, Spitalfields City Farm; Kate Johnson, Parklands Children's Centre; Ruth Kerr, Milestones, Hampshire's Living History Museum; Philip Knowling and Michelle Youd, Paignton Zoo; Hana Kovler, Mary Sambrook Children's Centre; Michelle Lee, Hill House St Mary's School; Lucy Micklethwait; Angela Moss, Sticky Fingers Playgroup, Caehopkins School; Jude Noble, Walkergate Early Years Centre; Amanda Phillips, Leeds City Art Gallery; Sally Pointer, Somerset House Nursery School; Julie Quinn; Wendy Redman, SEARCH, Hampshire Museums' Hands-On Centre; Rachel Riggs, Dynamic New Animation; Caroline Sloan, St Bernard's Nursery; Lesley Silvera, Hadrian's Wall Tourism Partnership; Kathryn Solly, Chelsea Open Air Nursery School; Jackie Sorrell, Woodmansterne Primary School; Ben Spencer, CABE Education; Emma Spencer; Nina Swann, Discovery, London Symphony Orchestra; Iona Towler-Evans; Naomi Wager.

We are particularly grateful for the invaluable help provided by the following people:

Alison Chapman; Richard Kearns; Rachel Salaman; William Salaman; June O'Sullivan, Maureen Wale and Marion Breslin, Westminster Children's Society; and the children from Hyde Park Barracks Nursery and Charing Cross Road Nursery, Westminster Children's Society; Jude Bowen and Charlotte Saunders of Paul Chapman Publishing and Michelle and Bill Antrobus of Deer Park Productions.

HOW TO USE THIS BOOK

This book will help you plan and run educational visits to different visitor attractions and the built environment. It offers a range of participative activities you can undertake at your setting before and after the visit, and, where practical, activities you can do with children at the chosen destination.

The suggested activities have been designed to support children's learning at Foundation Stage, with links to the Early Learning Goals specified at the end of each chapter. Practitioners at Key Stage 1 will also find this book useful. The activities are appropriate for children's learning at this level, and can be linked to the Key Stage 1 National Curriculum. The activities can be extended at your discretion to suit the children's learning levels, in particular through creative writing and scientific enquiry. Activities offer cross-curricular opportunities across the subject areas at both Foundation Stage and Key Stage 1. Case studies provide examples of visits made by different settings and descriptions of activities offered by certain venues. You can use these case studies to inform your own activities when planning a visit.

The book focuses on five types of environments which can be enjoyed by young children and help them learn. These are: museums; art galleries; performing arts venues; the built environment; and zoos, farms and aquariums. The book has been written to encourage you to access these provisions locally. The major museums, galleries, arts venues and other mainstream attractions rarely feature in this book because their excellence is well known. The museum or farm nearest your setting may not be renowned throughout the country, but nevertheless it may hold rich learning resources and valuable cross-curricular opportunities for children. The United Kingdom is fortunate in being particularly prolific in the number of visitor attractions it offers, in comparison to the vast majority of other countries around the globe. On your doorstep there will be venues which hold the key to provoking curiosity and delight in young children. This book will help you access those venues.

We have written this book with the firm belief that children's learning develops through exploring the opportunities offered at visitor attractions and in the built environment. The different destinations included in this book all share the same quality: they offer children learning opportunities through first-hand experiences, be these with objects, paintings, the performing arts, the built environment, or live animals. Pre-visit activities usefully prepare the children for the visit, and heighten their experience when they engage first-hand with the objects, animals or other stimuli encountered. Children's experiences at the venue are immediate and often exciting, motivating their interest. This can lead to vivid recollections which, when nurtured effectively, directly benefit children's learning after the excursion has taken place. The different learning opportunities suggested in this book seek to ensure space and time for child-initiated learning, with activities evolving and developing through the children's own explorations and discoveries.

Regular visits can become part of children's daily experience, rather than being one-off events outside their general learning. Frequent exposure to the multi-sensory opportunities offered by visitor attractions holds obvious benefits for children's learning. However, children will also become more confident through leaving their setting regularly, and will develop in their personal, social and emotional skills as a result. Children's regard for safety, for the other children in their group, and for the resources they will encounter will contribute to this area of their learning. This book includes the practical considerations required for any successful visit. If you ensure that the excursion runs smoothly, you will enable children to grow in confidence and to actively enjoy accessing the learning opportunities offered to them.

Inevitably, there are omissions in this book. The chapter exploring different performing arts is limited by necessity, and focuses on four areas of art forms (dance and movement, music, drama and mime, and puppetry). There are some wonderful learning opportunities available in historic houses, hands-on discovery centres and nature reserves. These venues are not included here. However, the intention is that you can adapt many of the activities in this book to complement visits to a range of different visitor attractions.

The book refers to any centre for the under-eights as *the setting*. This includes local authority nurseries, nursery centres, playgroups, pre-schools, childminder environments, schools in the independent, private and voluntary sectors, and maintained schools. The adults who work with children in the settings, whatever their qualifications, are termed *practitioners*. Occasional reference is made to *parents*. The word is used to include mothers, fathers, legal guardians and the primary carers of children in public care.

We hope that you will enjoy the activities and ideas offered in this book. More importantly, we hope that the book will encourage you to make visits regularly and easily. Young children are as entitled to access cultural opportunities as anyone else. You have the opportunity to enable this in an informed, safe and enjoyable context.

Visiting Museums

How museums can help young children learn

There is vast potential for young children to learn from the objects displayed in museums, and this learning tends to be immediate, because it doesn't require reading or writing. Objects in museum collections are becoming increasingly accessible for handling, providing additional rich learning opportunities for all children.

The real thing: Museums offer unique opportunities for children to engage with authentic objects. This enables children to understand immediately principles which might have been only available to them previously through verbal descriptions or pictures in books. You could show children in your setting an illustration of a brontosaurus, for example, but the sheer scale of the creature will only be evident when the children are face to face with a skeleton of the real thing.

Every object tells a story: Objects on display in museums are there for a reason, either because they are special in some way or because they represent part of a larger story. A limitless number of stories can emerge from any collection of objects, and you can adapt them to suit your own topics. Although objects provide rich opportunities to learn about real facts, stories about objects can also be imaginative. Carefully facilitated investigation and questioning can produce from children creative ideas about the object's provenance, how it was made and who owned it.

A sense of time: Objects can reveal much about different cultures, reflecting how people lived, worked and played. Objects held in museums come usually from the past, which can introduce to children a sense of time. Archaeological objects are often the only existing record of past cultures.

How things work: Many objects invite questions about their mechanical workings. These questions might be immediate, with large objects such as a plough or working steam engine, or come after close inspection, with objects which can be handled. Understanding how objects function can reveal a way of life that may have been unknown to children previously.

Patterns and decoration: Many objects in museums are visually stimulating, and can prompt discussion about the way patterns are designed and realized. This can lead to creative making activities, exploring colour and the use of different materials. In addition, cultural differences can be enjoyed through experiencing new and different types of decoration.

Language development: The excitement that children show when introduced to different artefacts is often expressed verbally. Attentive adults can encourage children's comments about what they are discovering, and introduce new vocabulary during these discussions.

Before the visit

Familiarization visit

It is highly recommended that you visit the museum before you take the children. This will enable you to become familiar with the collections on display, and to talk to an appropriate member of staff from the museum. Many museums employ education officers. If this is not the case with the museum you intend to visit, there will almost certainly be a staff member responsible for assisting groups visiting with an educational purpose. Talking to the designated person will give you an idea of how much support is provided by the museum for visiting groups of young children, as this can vary enormously. There may be an organized programme or there may be no provision at all. In some cases there is a set period of time for groups to explore the displays at their own pace, followed by organized workshops. At the very least, finding out how big the museum is and becoming familiar with the collections will result in a more informed visit for the children. It will also help you plan how long you will spend there.

Activities in the setting

Learning through objects can be encouraged at almost any time at your setting, and the activities suggested below are not necessarily exclusive to when you have organized a visit to a museum. However, if you do have a visit planned, there are a number of ways you can enable a deeper experience before you go.

Feely bags

You will need:

- Several fabric bags, each with a drawstring.

- A collection of objects. These can range from dolls and other toys, to functional household items such as cups and wooden spoons.

This is a simple and enjoyable activity which involves putting a number of objects into different bags, and letting the children guess what the objects are by feeling them. It can be played with just one child or with a large group of children sitting in a circle. Once at the museum, you can remind children of the feely bags activity when looking at the displays, asking the children to imagine what an item might feel like if it was in a bag.

Case Study 1 presents some questions you can ask the children as they feel the object. Once the object has been identified you can discuss it in more detail with the children; for example, you can talk about how it was used and how old the children think it might be. This activity doesn't need to be based on facts. Children can come up with very imaginative reasons why an object is like it is, and creative suggestions can be encouraged.

Case Study 1

SEARCH, Hampshire Museums' Hands-On Centre

SEARCH offers a range of activities for visiting groups of children, including **feely bags**. These can be reproduced at your setting, using any safe objects of your choice. SEARCH suggests the following prompts which the adult facilitator can say as children are feeling the object inside the bag.

- Put your hands inside the bag.
- No peeping!
- What does the object feel like?
- Is it rough or smooth?
- Is it hard or soft?
- Is it heavy or light?
- Is it furry?
- Do you know what it is?

Activity extensions:

- The child who feels the object can mime how it is used.

- Once the object has been revealed, further words can be used to describe what it looks like. For younger children you can offer choices such as 'What colours can you see?' or 'Is it plain or patterned?' Older children can offer words of their own to describe it.

- Once all the objects have been picked out of the bag, the children can group them in different ways. For instance, they can be grouped into kitchen items, toys, wooden things, plastic things, things with red in them, or things without red in them. There is no right or wrong way to group them.

Case Study 2

Object handling with a special needs class
Frogwell Primary School, Chippenham

This case study describes a handling session, with children with special needs from Frogwell Primary School led by a member of staff from Chippenham Museum.

There are children with a complex mix of Special Educational Needs (SEN) in the class, ranging from autism, visual impairment, different syndromes including Down's, to physical impairments such as hemiplegia. Some of the children have severe SEN so they need a high level of hands-on stimulus. The session is conducted with between nine and twelve children ranging in ages from 4 to 10 years.

The education officer comes to the setting with objects relevant to the current study theme. For example, if the theme is The Home, the museum worker will bring in antique domestic items. If the theme is Light, the objects will include lamps, candles, tallow and candlesticks. Handling sessions can also include relevant songs, like 'Four and twenty blackbirds' in the session on the home and 'Wee Willy Winkie' for the session on light.

The education officer, Jean, has become familiar to and with the children through termly visits. This contributes to the success of the session. Their interest kindled by the objects, the children spontaneously offer comments and ask questions. Jean and the teacher, Julie, have become a 'double act', where Julie can simplify things if necessary, adapting questions according to the abilities of the child. All the language used is backed up by visual and tactile stimuli.

The children get excited when the items are produced one by one out of a bag, because until then they have remained hidden like treasure. However, this stage of the activity must be timed appropriately to avoid confusion or over-stimulation; the children are only able to attend to one object at a time. This avoids a risk of the magic of the session being lost.

The session is successful because objects are real, and engagement with the objects for the children is first-hand. They can grasp the meaning of the object immediately. The session can last up to an hour, but will vary according to the children's concentration. The length of the session is dictated by the level of interest displayed by the children. The Light handling session continued after the children's break-time, as the children knew there were more items in the bag and wanted to find out what these were.

During the session Julie takes a photo of each child while they are holding an object. These photos are then made into a book. This serves as a useful recall tool for later prompting, as well as for reinforcing the learning. When the children look through the book they make comments in response to Julie's prompts, and the comments are typed up and added to the book.

The fact that Jean is a visitor from the nearby museum makes the session all the more exciting for the children. This also provides an opportunity for the teacher to observe the children responding to stimuli, a rare occurrence in the busy setting. However, Julie believes that it would still be of great interest to the children if Early Years practitioners conducted the session themselves. The focus of the session is the objects, not the facilitator.

Focus on …

Focusing on one object using several different approaches can prompt a whole range of creative activities, and can develop children's knowledge and understanding in a number of areas. A useful guide to follow when exploring objects with the children divides object exploration into four areas of questioning:

- What does it look like? (Form)
- What is it for? (Function)
- What is it made of? (Material)
- Where does it come from? (Provenance)

You can use a variety of enjoyable methods and media to investigate these areas with the children.

Object focus activities: clothes

Clothes offer rich learning opportunities when explored using the four areas of focus listed above, complementing several elements of the national curriculum. In addition, because everyone wears clothes, children will be able to identify with the theme immediately and make comparisons. However, clothes can also be different enough for the children to take an interest in them without referring to themselves. This ability to appreciate things objectively is a healthy and necessary part of children's self-development at this stage in their learning, and is a key factor to bear in mind when taking children to museums.

Some of the following activities, although based on a garment, have been designed so that any object of your choice can be explored in the same ways.

What's in the box?

You will need:

- A box, basket or chest
- A diverse range of items of clothing from hats to dresses to shoes

Fill a box with items of clothing. Include familiar garments that are recognizable everyday wear, garments with a cultural identity that reflect the ethnic make-up of the class, and unusual garments that are not familiar.

Sit the children in a circle and start by chanting the following rhyme to the tune of 'Row, row, row the boat':

What's, what's in the box? (We)

Mustn't let it drop.

Slowly passing, slowly passing,

Now it's time to stop!

All participants sing this as the box is passed around the circle. Whoever has it on the 'stop' will be the first to open the box and pull out a garment.

Questions to consider when the first garment is pulled out:

■ How do you put it on? (This shows how it might be worn.)

■ Where's it from? (You could look at the label for clues.)

■ Who does it belong to? (This can be set up with a garment which is easily identifiable, or as a guessing game with no right answer required.)

■ Who can see something else in this room which looks similar? (For example, in colour, pattern or shape.)

Photo gallery/fashion magazine

You will need:

■ A digital camera

■ A basket

■ Clothes for dressing up (include a variety of familiar and unfamiliar, dressing-up and everyday wear, collected by staff and parents)

■ A catwalk stage in the role-play area for photograph posing

■ An album for a magazine

■ A display area for the gallery

Using a digital camera for this activity works well, as the results are immediate. Allow the children to take the photos of each other because they can be intuitive about capturing each other's moments of discovery.

Children can try on clothes and adopt a pose in response to what they are wearing. Photographs can be taken in different areas of the setting or outside. During the activity, discuss with the children the function and the material of the clothes. The children can also give names to their outfits as they invent new characters.

Group together the photographs as a gallery display or a magazine, and show them with quotes taken from the children's spoken descriptions of the clothes they chose.

Catwalk show

You will need a role-play area which includes:

■ Clothes (a variety of familiar and unfamiliar, dressing-up and everyday wear, collected by staff and parents)

■ A catwalk stage

1.1 Catwalk show, Hyde Park Barracks Nursery

- A long mirror

- Spotlights (anglepoise lamps can work just as well)

- Disco lights (these can be purchased cheaply from various 'pound shops')

- Music stereo with a selection of CDs

- A changing area

- A clothes horse

- Chairs along the catwalk

- A writing area for invitations, posters, brochures

- A microphone for the compère

Create a fashion show role-play area in the setting which incorporates a changing area, a catwalk stage, mirrors, lights and music. You could also include a microphone for the compère.

Children can try on combinations of clothing according to the clothes' colour and material, and walk in the clothes to the rhythm of the music. Ask the children questions while they are dressing up and moving to the music. How does the garment respond to the movement? Is the garment heavy or light? Have the colours of the garment changed in the light?

You can discuss with the children why they have chosen to wear particular garments, and the nature of each garment's style, function, colour and pattern. The group could also discuss the history of the garments – where they came from, who they belong to and how they were acquired.

Role-play areas

Creating imaginative role-play areas will support and encourage learning through child-initiated play. This needs to incorporate positive and strong adult engagement to challenge the thinking of the children as they play with the clothes.

Suggested role-play areas:

- Clothes shop

- Launderette

- Hat shop

- Jumble sale

Consider the following as prompts for learning:

- Buying clothes according to preference of colour, material, pattern and function.

- Pricing clothes according to the above.

- Displaying them – how to hang, fold and lay out the clothes according to the garments' material and function.

Preparing activity sheets

If there is little or no formalized Early Years provision at the museum, you may want to develop some yourself. This depends on your pre-visit familiarization of the museum. You can arrange a simple 'finding' activity for the children by drawing or taking photos of five objects during this familiarization visit. These can be reproduced on paper, and the children's task can be to seek out the items. A sample activity sheet from Milestones Museum in Hampshire is provided here. This type of activity works well when complemented by encouragement and discussion from adult facilitators.

Activity sheets can be adapted according to the ages and abilities of the children at your setting. Some children may enjoy the challenge of finding objects using one tiny detail as a clue. Younger children may enjoy going on a 'colour hunt', as suggested by Milestones Museum in Case Study 3.

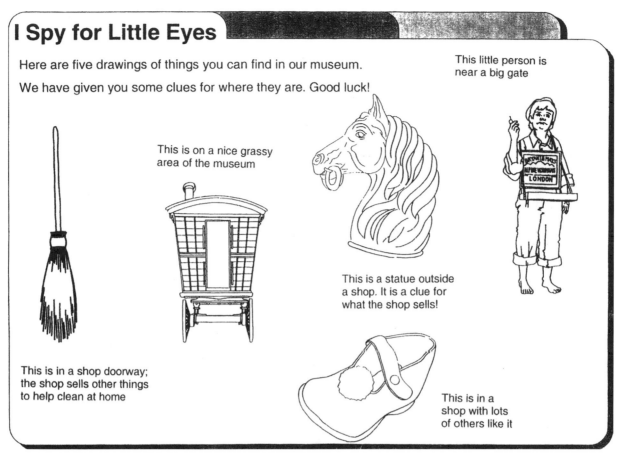

I Spy for Little Eyes

Here are five drawings of things you can find in our museum.

We have given you some clues for where they are. Good luck!

This little person is near a big gate

This is on a nice grassy area of the museum

This is a statue outside a shop. It is a clue for what the shop sells!

This is in a shop doorway; the shop sells other things to help clean at home

This is in a shop with lots of others like it

1.2 *I Spy* activity sheet, Milestones, Hampshire's Living History Museum

Reproduced with kind permission from Milestones, Hampshire's Living History Museum.

Briefing the adult helpers

After your initial familiarization visit, you will be able to brief other adults about the layout of the space and the nature of the collections. It will also help you to offer ideas for questions that adults might ask if they see a child in their group taking an interest in a particular object or collection of objects.

On the day

The following activities are suggested for Early Years groups that have time to explore the museum collections by themselves.

Observation

The activity sheets described on page 8 can encourage children to become familiar and at ease with the objects on display, as well as refining their observational skills. Giving each child a magnifying glass or 'spy glass' can encourage further observation.

I spy

This activity can work with any number of children. It is a good 'warm-up' game, as it enables the children to become familiar with the space and the objects on display.

This simple, observation-based activity is easy to conduct, as children are likely to know the principle of 'I spy'. Milestones Museum (see case study below) provided sheets for the visiting group to use. However, this is something you can provide yourself, as suggested in the Preparing activity sheets section above, page 8, or you can play the game just as easily by looking and speaking.

Run the activity near a display which has a number of different objects within it. The examples given here focus on the four ways of exploring objects outlined on page 5: what they look like, what they are for, what they are made of and where they come from. Younger children find it easier to concentrate on what an object looks like and what it is used for.

- I spy with my little eye, something which has a handle on it.

- I spy with my little eye, something which can pour out tea.

- I spy with my little eye, something which will break if you drop it as it's made of china.

- I spy with my little eye, something which comes from a kitchen or dining room.

Encourage everyone in the group to have a go at choosing an object. The activity is also effective in motivating children to name the object when they think they know which it is. They will need to search for the word 'teapot', for example, and if they don't know it, they can use other describing words to indicate which object they have identified.

Case Study 3

Museum visit to Milestones, Hampshire's Living History Museum

St Bernard's Nursery, Basingstoke

Twenty-eight children aged between 2 and 5 years old visited Milestones Museum as part of their work on the topic of Transport. They travelled to the museum by bus, and investigated the museum's displays in groups of seven, accompanied by adult helpers from the nursery. The gallery visited is called the Post Office, and is funded by Hampshire County Council's Adult and Community Learning Unit. The nursery manager had visited the museum beforehand to familiarize herself with the displays and with aspects of health and safety. This enabled her to brief the accompanying adults before the visit.

The simple **I spy** sheets provided by the museum proved an enjoyable and effective way of engaging even the youngest children with the exhibits. The children quickly understood the game after spying the first object on the sheets, and were motivated to look carefully at the displays for the other items pictured. The 2-year-olds particularly enjoyed spotting the colours on the real objects. When the groups found the objects, the accompanying adult talked with them about how each object might have been used.

The nursery has since built in an annual visit to the museum as part of their Transport topic, as they have seen how the children can understand the concepts of time and history more immediately in the museum than through any description or pictures. Travelling to the museum by bus also provides children with a good comparison of old and new vehicles which they can relate to using their own direct experience.

Discussion

Sensitive and informed adult help can greatly enhance a museum visit for young children. The adults will need to direct their questions in specific areas for this to be successful. The four ways of looking at objects described on page 5 provide guidelines for this. The adults can encourage the children to think about the object they are interested in according to what it looks like, what it's for, what it's made of and where it comes from. Below are some sample questions for the four different areas which you could give to adult helpers to use during the museum visit.

What the object looks like:

- How many colours can you see? What are they?

- What's your favourite colour on the (object), and why?

- Can you see any shapes? What are they?

- Can you see anything else in the museum which is like this?

- Do you have anything at home which looks like this?

What the object is for:

- What do you think this was used for?

- How do you think it works? (Discussion around the main components of the object.)

- Do you think it looks easy or difficult to use?

- Have you got anything like this at home?

What the object is made of:

- What do you think it's made of?

- Does it look smooth or rough?

- Do you think it looks light or heavy?

- Have you got anything at home which reminds you of this?

Where the object comes from:

- Who do you think owned this before it came to the museum? (Imaginative answers can be encouraged.)

- Do you think this is very old, or quite new? (Discussion around the notion of new things and old things.)

- Do you think this had to travel a long way to get to the museum? How do you think it got here?

Simple questions can lead to detailed discussion. However, it is also important to allow children the time and space to get to know an object which captures their interest without the adult pouncing on them with questions. The unobtrusive presence of an adult may well be enough to prompt children to share their thoughts.

Drawing

There may be opportunities within a museum for children to deepen their responses through drawing activities. These may be kept very simple, with you providing plain paper and coloured pencils if the children want them. Clipboards are also useful in this context, as museums are often carpeted. Alternatively, you can initiate an organized drawing activity by encouraging children to find one object in the museum that they like, which they can then draw and colour. This activity also provides a good opportunity to create a display in your own setting which records the visit through the children's eyes.

Before your visit, check with the museum's education officer that drawing activities are allowed in the museum space.

1.3 Handling bones at the Museum of London

Sharing ideas

This activity encourages observation and communication. Ask each of the children to choose their favourite object from what they have seen during the museum visit. Put the children into pairs. One child of the pair shows their partner the object they have selected, and, depending on the age of the participating children, tells their partner why they like it. The children then swap over and follow the same procedure. When the children are gathered together in the group, each child is asked to report on what their partner chose, and why they liked the chosen object.

This activity depends on the children remembering what their partner shared with them, so it is best conducted while still at the museum. The activity can be extended by allowing each child to take a photo of their partner's chosen object. These photos will serve as an aide-mémoire in further discussion, and create the potential for a display.

Victoria and Albert Museum visit

Hyde Park Barracks Nursery, Westminster Children's Society (WCS)

Children at Hyde Park Barracks Nursery visit museums frequently. Each trip is usually preceded by a member of the nursery's staff visiting the displays beforehand and bringing back postcards to show the children. This builds a sense of anticipation and offers opportunities for children to discuss the themes of the displays before the visit takes place.

Ten children aged 3 and 4 visited the Victoria and Albert Museum's Dress Collection with three accompanying adults. The group first walked around the displays, discussing what they could see. The children were interested in the patterns on the costumes, commenting on the 'bells' (bluebells) and 'roses' printed on the fabric. After looking at the collection, the children chose their favourite costumes and drew them from observation, using coloured pencils.

During the visit, the group looked a woman's dress which was very wide and long. This dialogue shows how the lead practitioner linked the costumes to experiences in the children's everyday life.

Practitioner: Where do you think she's going?

Isabella: To a party.

Michael: Or to a ball.

Practitioner: If she came and visited us in the nursery, how do you think she would get through the door?

Maggie: She'd get her dress caught.

Aaron: She could climb in through the window.

Blanca: She could fall down the stairs, because that dress is too long.

The children start looking at a slender blue dress next to the pink dress.

Matthew (pointing to the blue dress): I bet **she** can get through the door.

When you are at the museum, notice what interests the children and find out if postcards or posters of the objects can be bought at the museum shop. These provide very useful resources once back at your setting.

After the visit

Art activities can be an effective way to consolidate the children's visit to the museum, enabling them to respond creatively to the things they have seen and possibly handled. The following suggested activities explore the visual elements of art: line; tone; pattern; texture; colour; shape;

form and space. Three-dimensional sculpture and printing can be used as follow-up activities to the visit, if the materials and resources are available and if an adult is present to give support in a non-directed atmosphere. You can adapt these activities so that they suit the objects and collections which the children looked at during their museum visit.

3D model-making: salt dough sculpture

You will need:

- Plain flour

- Salt

- Food colour (coloured ink is a vivid alternative but it does stain)

- Water

The salt dough can be made using the proportions three parts plain flour and to one part salt. Mix in water and food colour to create the consistency of soft dough. You can use the salt dough mixture for up to two days, if necessary softening it by kneading.

For decoration:

- Pulses, seeds, beans

- Shape pasta (these could be sprayed gold and silver)

- Rice (this can be coloured with food colour)

You can sustain and extend children's interests in three-dimensional objects by encouraging them to respond to tactile qualities. When children explore in three dimensions they experiment with a range of sensations which increase their understanding of how things are made and what they feel like.

The activity is enhanced if you have a postcard, photograph or poster of a three-dimensional object which the children enjoyed looking at during their visit. Before they begin, show them the postcard or poster and discuss with them what they noticed about the object in the museum. What was it made of? Do they think it would feel smooth or rough? Is it curved, or does it have straight edges? After talking about the object, the children can tear off a chunk of the dough, experiment through manipulating it, and create their own interpretation of the object. Use pulses, seeds, beans and pasta to add decorative features. If you want to harden the finished works, you can place them next to a radiator or in an airing cupboard, or put them overnight in an oven which has been switched off and is cooling down.

Textiles: paste resist

This activity is enriched if you have a postcard or photograph of an object that the children have seen at the museum. It can work well when referring to patterned clothes, and to ceramic objects which have a coloured background and a white design. Patterns on the object can also provide inspiration for the children's own designs.

You will need:

- White fabric (it's good to experiment with different types of material to achieve a variety of results)

- Fabric dye, put into spray bottles or paint pots (this is permanent dye, so ensure the children's clothes are well covered to enable them to experiment freely with it)

- Masking tape to hold the material taut

- A flat drying space

A variety of resist materials:

- Paste resist: flour and water

- Washing-up liquid

- PVA glue

- Washing powder

- White chalk or oil pastels

Paste resist is an alternative to batik. Mix up flour and water to the consistency of pancake mixture so it can be squeezed out of a washing-up liquid bottle. The paste needs to be very smooth as lumps can clog up the nozzle. You can squeeze out patterns on to pieces of fabric and then spray colour over the fabric when the paste resist is dry. Alternatively, you can spray colour over the material while the squeezed-out patterns are still wet; both ways are effective. Breaking and peeling off the dried paste is the final part of the process, which leaves behind the white relief.

The alternative resists listed below don't require breaking and peeling off at the end of the process, unlike the paste resist.

- Washing-up liquid. Dribble small amounts from pipettes or small squeezy bottles in patterns on to the surface of the fabric. This leaves a lovely translucent effect when food colour or very diluted paint is put all over the fabric. The colour needs to be applied while the washing-up liquid is still wet.

- PVA glue. Dilute the glue with water and apply with brushes or glue sticks. Dripping this on to the material works well as a resist technique, and when it dries it leaves a shiny hard line. Cover the rest of the fabric with fabric dye using the spray bottle.

- Washing powder. Mix with water to make a thick paste and apply it with paint brushes. Spray colour all over the fabric.

- White chalk or oil pastel. This can be a small-scale and finer way to achieve the resist effect. The white marks will remain if you first apply the chalk or oil pastel on to the material and then spray colour all over the fabric.

Rub collages

For this activity you can either base the artwork on a postcard or photograph of an object which the children have enjoyed looking at in the museum, or you can provide a real object of your own. The activity will heighten children's appreciation of the shape and decoration of an object.

You will need:

- Sugar paper

- Scissors

- Printing ink (washable printing ink is available from educational suppliers)

- Ink trays

- Rollers

- Paper to print on (it's good to experiment with a variety of different types of paper)

- Crayons and pastels

On a piece of sugar paper, draw the shape of the chosen object, for example a vase, and cut it out. On another piece of sugar paper, draw and then cut out the features which can be seen on the object, for example the geometric shapes decorating the vase. Stick these features on to the piece of paper which is in the shape of the object. You can then either roll printing ink on to the work and press the inked cut-out on to a fresh piece of paper, or place a thin sheet of paper over the cut-out and rub it with a crayon. The finished artwork will be a print showing shape and pattern, and can be displayed alongside the postcard or photograph of the object which was used for the activity.

Our own museum

Clear a space in the setting which can represent a museum display. Objects can be selected from the setting, but it's more involving for children if you ask them to bring from their home any item which they think would be interesting to display in the museum. Once the objects have been collected, encourage the children to think of a simple museum label. This could show just the object's name, or it could include, for example, whom it belongs to and how it has been used. Children can write and create their own labels with a variety of mark-making tools, such as felt-tip pens, chalks and crayons, with help from the supporting adult only if necessary. Encourage the children to make their labels sturdier by sticking them on to card. A smaller triangular piece of card can be stuck upright on the back so that the label stands up.

When the labels have been prepared, ask the children to lay the objects out with the labels next to them in the arranged space. You can extend the activity by asking the children to group the objects so that they are arranged in themes of the children's choosing. Additional labels can be produced to explain the nature of the themes.

Curriculum Links

1 Feely bags

2 What's in the box?

3 Photo gallery

4 Catwalk show

5 Role-play areas

6 I spy

7 Drawing

8 Sharing ideas

9 3D model-making: salt dough sculpture

10 Textile colour relief

11 Rub collages

12 Our own museum

Early Learning Goals	Activity	Area of Learning
Continue to be interested, excited and motivated to learn.	All	PSE: Dispositions and attitudes
Be confident to try out new activities, indicate ideas and speak in a familiar group.	1, 2, 5, 6	
Maintain attention, concentrate, and sit quietly when appropriate.	1, 2, 6	
Respond to significant experiences, showing a range of feelings when appropriate.	4, 5	PSE: Self-confidence and self-esteem
Have a developing awareness of their own needs, views and feelings and be sensitive to the needs, views and feelings of others.	2, 5	
Have a developing respect for their own cultures and beliefs and those of others.	8	
Form good relationships with adults and peers.	4, 5, 8	PSE: Making relationships
Work as part of a group or class, taking turns and sharing fairly, understanding that there needs to be agreed values and codes of behaviour for groups of people, including adults and children, to work together harmoniously.	1, 2, 3, 4, 5	
Understand that people have different needs, views, cultures and beliefs, that need to be treated with respect.	8	PSE: Sense of community
Understand that they can expect others to treat their needs, views, cultures and beliefs with respect.	8	

▶

Early Learning Goals	Activity	Area of Learning
Interact with others, negotiating plans and activities and taking turns in conversation.	2, 5, 6, 8	CLL: Language for communication
Enjoy listening to and using spoken and written language, and readily turn to it in their play and learning.	4, 5, 12	
Sustain attentive listening, responding to what they have heard by relevant comments, questions or actions.	2, 6, 8	
Extend their vocabulary, exploring the meanings and sounds of new words.	1, 2, 6, 9	
Speak clearly and audibly with confidence and control and show awareness of the listener, for example by their use of conventions such as greetings, 'please' and 'thank you'.	4	
Use language to imagine and recreate roles and experiences.	1, 2, 4, 5	CLL: Language for thinking
Use talk to organize, sequence and clarify thinking, ideas, feelings and events.	1, 2, 8	
Attempt writing for different purposes, using features of different forms such as lists, stories and instructions.	5, 12	CLL: Writing
Write their own names and other things such as labels and captions and begin to form simple sentences, sometimes using punctuation.	5, 12	
Use developing mathematical ideas and methods to solve practical problems.	5	MD: Numbers as labels and for counting
In practical activities and discussion begin to use the vocabulary involved in adding and subtracting.	5	MD: Calculating
Use language such as 'greater', 'smaller', 'heavier' or 'lighter' to compare quantities.	1, 6, 9	MD: Shape, space and measure
Use language such as 'circle' or 'bigger' to describe the shape and size of solids and flat shapes.	1, 2, 6, 9	
Use everyday words to describe position.	5	
Investigate objects and materials by using all their senses as appropriate.	1, 3, 4, 6, 7, 9, 12	KNU: Exploration and investigation
Find out more about and identify some features of living things, objects and events they observe.	1, 6, 8, 9	
Look closely at similarities, differences, patterns and change.	2, 8	
Ask questions about why things happen and how things work.	6	

Early Learning Goals	Activity	Area of Learning
Build and construct with a wide range of objects, selecting appropriate resources, and adapting their work where necessary.	4, 5	KNU: Designing and making skills
Select the tools and techniques they need to shape, assemble and join materials they are using.	5, 10	
Find out about and identify the uses of everyday technology and use information and communication technology and programmable toys to support their learning.	3, 4, 5	KNU: Information and communication technology
Find out about past and present events in their own lives, and those of their families and other people they know.	2, 10	KNU: Sense of time
Observe, find out about and identify features in the place they live and the natural world.	5, 6	KNU: Sense of place
Move with confidence, imagination and safety.	4, 5	PD: Movement
Move with control and co-ordination.	4, 9, 10	
Show awareness of space, of themselves and of others.	4, 5	PD: Sense of space
Use a range of small and large equipment.	5	PD: Using equipment
Handle tools, objects, construction and malleable materials safely and with increasing control.	1, 9, 10	PD: Using tools and materials
Explore colour, texture, shape, form, space in two or three dimensions.	1, 2, 6, 7, 8, 9, 10, 11	CD: Exploring media and materials
Use their imagination in art and design, music, dance, imaginative and role play and stories.	4, 5, 9, 10, 11	CD: Imagination
Respond in a variety of ways to what they see, hear, smell, touch and feel.	1, 2, 5, 6, 9, 10, 11	CD: Responding to experiences, and expressing and communicating ideas
Express and communicate their ideas, thoughts and feelings by using a widening range of materials, suitable tools, imaginative and role play, movement, designing and making, and a variety of songs and musical instruments.	3, 5, 7, 9, 10, 11	

CHAPTER 2

Visiting Art Galleries

This chapter is divided into the following sections:

■ How art galleries can help young children learn

■ Before the visit

■ On the day

■ After the visit

This chapter often refers to paintings, but the approaches suggested may be equally relevant for drawings, sculptures and most other art forms displayed in galleries.

How art galleries can help young children learn

Close observation of content-rich subject matter: Detailed observation of paintings can extend children's skills in understanding narrative, characters, places, shapes, colours and the past.

Inspiration and creativity: Paintings can provide a rich source of creative inspiration for children when making their own artwork. For example, they may see new uses of everyday materials in contemporary art or notice the rich use of colours in paintings or prints. Media like charcoal and pastels can be used well by young children, even more so when they see examples from art on display. Seeing how artists deal with a particular subject matter can also give children new ideas for the subject matter of their own creative work.

Language development: Looking at art in an art gallery can enthuse and motivate children to talk about what they see. Children's curiosity can lead to new describing words. Oil paintings can appear 'shiny' or 'glossy' and the prolific use of colour in paintings offers opportunities for adjectives such as 'cherry red' or 'apple green'. Looking at paintings can also inspire stories, songs and rhymes.

Cross-curricular learning: Paintings can also be used to support everyday teaching within the setting, providing enjoyable and refreshing illustrations of subjects covered within all areas of the Foundation Stage. Ideas for this are suggested towards the end of this chapter.

Before the visit

Familiarization visit

It will make all the difference to your visit with the children if you familiarize yourself with the art gallery beforehand. As you work on a particular topic, you can use your preliminary visit to select particular paintings that you will highlight when you return with the children.

Many art galleries employ a designated member of staff to promote the educational potential of the collection. At the very least, there will be a member of staff who can advise you on practical aspects which will facilitate your visit with the children. There may also be programmes or workshops offered, which you could build into your visit, although it's worth making time to absorb the work on display at your own pace as well.

By visiting the art gallery before the arranged visit with the children, you will be able to run focused activities specific to chosen paintings. Reproductions of these paintings can be useful learning resources, even if they are only postcard size. When choosing specific paintings to focus on in the gallery shop, check that they will be on display when you come back with the children, as exhibits can be removed from time to time. If your budget allows, buy a number of reproductions of each painting, so that several children can look at the picture simultaneously in your setting. Ask the gallery what their policy is for photography, as you may be allowed to take photographs of works of art. It's best to focus on a maximum of three paintings, as it is unlikely that you will have time to look at more than this number when you visit the gallery with the children.

Some of the following activities assume that a familiarization visit has taken place. Others are more general.

Art I spy

This version of the game 'I spy' is a good introduction to looking at paintings generally, and it can be played using a reproduction of a picture in the setting before the visit. The activity can also work well when played during your visit to the art gallery.

Choose one detail or more from your chosen paintings to be the subject of the game. Examples might include:

- *I spy* … (a particular shape), for example, *I spy something in the shape of a triangle.*
- *I spy* … (a particular colour), for example, *I spy something which is light blue.*
- *I spy* … (a particular type of person, marked out by the way they are dressed), for example, *I spy a beggar.*
- *I spy* … (the number of times an object is depicted, which the group can then all count together), for example, *I spy five flowers in the field.*

This is a game for everyone to take turns in playing, and it can be easy or challenging to suit the age range and abilities within the group.

What's in the picture?

This activity encourages children to observe particular features of individual paintings. The picture you choose can be either a reproduction of something the children will see during their visit to the art gallery, or a painting chosen from a book.

Preparation

■ Make a colour wheel by cutting out a circular piece of white card. Draw three lines through the centre of the circle so that you have six equal sections. Colour these in so that you have segments of red, orange, yellow, green, blue and purple. Make an arrow out of card and place it so that the end without the arrowhead is in the centre of the card. Push a paper fastener through the end of the arrow and through the colour wheel itself, and fix the fastener so that there is still enough slack to spin the arrow.

■ Make a shapes wheel in the same way as described above, but this time divide the wheel into four equal sections, rather than six. Draw one shape in each quarter of the circle. Suitable shapes can be squares, triangles, circles and rectangles.

Activity

■ The children can take it in turns to spin the arrow and look at where it lands. They then need to refer to the picture you are holding and see if the colour or the shape can be found in it.

■ The colour wheel game is most effective with the younger children, who will enjoy matching the colour on the wheel to the painting. It helps if you can choose paintings which have many colours within them, to avoid potential disappointment if the wheel's colour is not featured.

■ The shapes wheel game can encourage the imaginations of older children, who may see a triangle shape in a church spire, or a circle shape in a person's face or a piece of fruit.

Noisy pictures

This activity can be great fun and works well during circle time. It needs an energetic adult to get the right mood going from the outset.

Preparation

You can either use reproductions of paintings you have seen during your familiarization visit to the art gallery or you can look through art books in your setting and pick out appropriate pictures. The paintings need to depict objects that make a noise in real life, for example trains, cars, babies or animals. If you are working from a book, mark the relevant pages with Post-its so that the activity can move along smoothly.

Activity

Explain to the children that this is a noisy game where everyone can be as loud as they like. Describe the premise of the game, which is to make the sound that would be made by the object pointed at in the picture. You can add to the game by asking the children to make up actions to go with their noises.

Show the children the reproduction of the first painting and ask them what they see. There may be more than one object in the painting that makes sounds in real life. Everyone needs to agree on the object for which they will make the relevant sounds or a cacophony will result! One way of doing this is to encourage children to take it in turns to choose an object, and then have everyone make the appropriate sounds.

If everyone is enjoying the game, you can play a quick version once all the paintings have been viewed and the sounds established. Revisit the pictures in a random order, at a fast pace. The children have to respond quickly by making the right sounds (and actions) as soon as they see the relevant object in the picture.

Art activities

Visiting an art gallery that shows contemporary art can provide a wonderful stimulus for children to try out related art activities in the setting, both before and after the visit. Case Study 5 describes the creative experimentation enjoyed by a group of children in their setting when working with artists. This is clearly an effective way for children's creativity to be nurtured by professionals. However, you shouldn't feel daunted if funding doesn't allow for your setting to employ an artist. There are many ideas and resources in books and on the Internet which can support you in this area.

A familiarization visit to view the contemporary art on display at the art gallery will give you ideas for setting-based activities, such as what materials the artists have used, the themes being addressed, and their use of line, shape and colour. Any or all of these elements can be explored creatively by the children in their own way, before their visit to the art gallery.

Case Study 5

Adventurous Ways, Leeds City Art Gallery

Several Early Years settings participated in the project Adventurous Ways, an element of the Being and Becoming programme devised by Leeds City Art Gallery. The project was funded by Sure Start, Education Leeds, and Space@Brackenedge. Artists Emma Spencer and Kate Jeneva facilitated the activities. The workshops taking place within the settings explored different aspects of the artwork on display at Leeds City Art Gallery. The children viewed these on a visit to the gallery, which formed an important part of the project. The activities described here took place in art rooms within the settings where the children could be free and messy when exploring their creative ideas.

Large-scale mark-making

This workshop explored the theme of journeys, and was stimulated by images of different objects related to the artwork on display at Leeds City Art Gallery. The workshop acted as an icebreaker and initiated thinking

Case Study *continued*

about line. One activity, called 'taking a line on a journey', involved children dripping paint randomly along the art room's floor after making a hole in the bottom of a cup and filling it with paint.

Large-scale projections of the gallery's artwork

The projections of the artwork showed the colours of the works and some places where the children could journey in their imagination. In a darkened room the projections created a colourful space to which the children responded creatively. They instantly immersed themselves in the projection, making swimming and dancing movements, and trying to 'capture' the image seen projected on to the clothes of other children. This activity served to introduce the artwork to the children in an exciting way.

Ribbon and wool lines

Lines found in the paintings in the art gallery were chosen for their colours, and the children selected ribbons and lengths of wool to match them. They took these 'lines' on journeys to produce three-dimensional structures, creating new artwork as a result. The workshop stimulated free play and storytelling. It additionally left something behind in the settings that could be used after the formal end of the project.

Three of the four participating settings carried on thinking about lines outside the project. One setting put large paper around the perimeter of their building and invited children to take a line on a journey. Another used the ribbon sculpture they had created to construct a den where storytelling took place. A third setting initiated a weaving activity as a new way of taking a line on a journey.

Briefing the adult helpers

As when planning a visit to a museum, your initial familiarization visit to the art gallery will be very useful when briefing adult helpers before the trip takes place. It will enable you to give them confidence about the layout of the space and the nature of the collections. It will also give you the opportunity to offer adult helpers ideas for prompt questions if a child in their group takes a particular interest in a work of art.

On the day

At the art gallery

The activities provided here have been designed for Early Years groups that have the time and opportunity to explore the art collections by themselves. Typically, a visit with young children will not exceed an hour, unless the children are thoroughly engaged. You can select from the activities below, rather than tackle them all. However, the hands-on activities will lengthen the children's attention spans and extend the visit in a meaningful and enjoyable way.

It's useful to bring along with you any reproductions you have been looking at with the children beforehand. This is so that children can point to features in the postcard or poster if they are unable to describe those features in the real painting.

Discussion is a valuable part of any visit to an art gallery. Children are naturally interested in looking at images and may interpret them in unexpected ways. These may be different from the artist's intention. For example, the children may interpret a strip of blue paint rendering light on a building as a river. It's up to you how you respond to the children's perceptions, but there is value in not contradicting or correcting them. Instead you could choose to go with the flow, encouraging the children to pursue their creative ideas further.

2.1 Parklands Early Years Centre's visit to Leeds City Art Gallery
Photograph taken with permission from Leeds City Art Gallery

Drawing

Giving young children the opportunity to draw from observation helps them to recreate life around them through their own eyes – a tradition which dates back to prehistoric times. Observational drawing also enables children to extend their attention span and to focus on individual components of a larger whole. This has great benefits for their learning in general.

Copying a painting in an art gallery will help children remember that painting for years to come. The activity gives children the time and space to observe a painting closely, whether it is the colour, line, form, or narrative which interests them. Their finished drawings will serve as an aide-mémoire and can be displayed later at the setting.

It is recommended that before your visit you check with staff at the art gallery to confirm that drawing activities are allowed in the space where the paintings are hung. Some galleries are relaxed about this and, provided the children are familiar with the particular art materials, may allow the use of media such as charcoal. Others may prefer only pencils to be used. Large sheets of plain paper will allow children the freedom to experiment with scale, although they will require something firm to place under the paper. You may need to bring these items with you to the gallery.

The accompanying adults can help children with this activity by talking with them as they draw, unobtrusively chatting about the things both the child and adult observe in the painting. Comments might focus on how the artist has rendered something. For example, 'Can you see how the tree is painted all the way from the bottom of the picture to the top of the picture?' However, children will decide for themselves how they choose to copy the painting. They are likely to pick out elements of the artwork rather than copy all of the features in the painting.

Pipe-cleaner poses

If you bring a bag of pipe-cleaners with you on your visit, you will find children use them in a huge variety of ways in response to the artworks on display. The pipe-cleaners can be used to echo shapes within paintings, including the poses of people and the shapes of trees. The longer pipe-cleaners are best for this activity. Avoid using sparkly pipe-cleaners, as the glitter on them has a tendency to fall on the floor. This will not make you very popular with the art gallery staff!

Treasure hunt

This activity requires a bit of preparation on your part, but it's always a favourite with children.

On your familiarization visit, pick out objects depicted in paintings that are available as the 'real thing'. Items could include a piece of fruit, a scarf, a stone or a plant. It depends on the paintings you have chosen for the activity. Collect the real items before your visit to the art gallery and put them in a drawstring bag.

When you are at the gallery, ask the children to feel inside the bag and find an object. See if they can recognize the object just by feeling it. If they can, they then need to find the painting in which that object is depicted. Younger children may want to look at the object in the bag first, and then find it in the painting.

Variation: matching materials

On your familiarization visit, look at the materials depicted in the paintings. There may be silk dresses, a metal helmet, a pearl necklace, a wooden boat, a stone wall or a fur stole. When you get back to the setting, see how many examples of those materials you can find, preferably in a simple, abstract form. For example, a little block of wood may be recognized quickly by a child as 'wood', but a wooden model of a car may be first viewed by a child as a car.

Place your samples of different materials into a drawstring bag. Children can pick out one of the materials after feeling it carefully while it is still in the bag. This is a good opportunity to talk with the children about what the material feels like, where describing words for textures can be used. The child can then find where the material is depicted in the painting.

Visit to the National Gallery, London

Charing Cross Road Nursery, Westminster Children's Society (WCS)

Children from Charing Cross Road Nursery make regular visits to galleries. They participate in any Early Years provision offered, but often their visits are led by nursery staff rather than gallery staff, such as the visit described here.

Preparation

The setting had been exploring buildings as their topic for the term, so the lead practitioner was keen to find paintings that featured buildings. She visited the gallery on her own to locate relevant paintings and chose three: **The Stonemason's Yard** by Canaletto, **Farms near Auvers** by Vincent van Gogh, and **Westminster Abbey** by Monet. Two of these were reproduced as postcards for sale in the shop, so she bought three of each to show the children before they visited the gallery themselves. She selected five children from the setting who she thought would benefit especially from the visit, and talked with them beforehand about the paintings they would be looking at. This group of five studied the postcard reproductions of the paintings, pointing out what they could see.

In advance of the visit, the practitioner gathered together different representative objects which featured in one of the paintings. These included a toy cockerel, a white stone, a plastic toy boat and some white cloth. She put these items in a drawstring bag. She also included in the bag some small geometric shapes and some plastic cubes of different colours. She chose the colours based on those featured in the second painting to be explored by the group during their visit.

Gallery visit

The five children were accompanied by three adults. The group sat in front of the first painting and the children responded to the questions asked by the lead practitioner. Time was allowed for the children to make their own comments. The children were interested in the people depicted in the foreground of the picture and spent some time discussing them:

- I can see a little girl rolling.
- I think she has fallen down.
- That's her mummy standing there.
- No, that's her daddy.
- Daddies are bigger and mummies are smaller.
- That's not true. Sometimes mummies are bigger.

The lead practitioner played 'I spy' with the children, where the children spotted the boats, the church, and the windows. The children then picked the prepared objects from the bag and found them in the picture. They also matched the shapes to features in the picture, linking the triangle representing the church spire and the square to the windows.

The children's concentration was lengthened by the discussion and the different games which were played in front of the first painting. Over 30 minutes was spent in front of that painting alone.

Colour quest

This is an effective activity for very young children. In preparation, gather fabric samples of different colours. Put the pieces of fabric into a drawstring bag and let the children take out one fabric sample each. Their task is to find the colour of the fabric in a nearby painting.

The activity can be repeated until each child has found a colour. Make sure you prepare enough fabric if you want all the children in your group to have a go at this activity. Encourage the children to talk about how each colour has been rendered in the painting, once they have located it. The colour might be bright, dark or light. It might dominate the painting or feature only slightly. The colour might make the child feel happy or scared. Discussions such as these can extend the children's vocabulary and develop their powers of observation.

Mirror mimicking

All this activity requires is a large hand-held mirror and some paintings showing people. Portraits are best, as they depict the facial expression in detail. This is an effective activity to engage a single child or a group of confident children.

Look at the chosen picture with the child or children and talk about the facial expression of the person depicted. Are they happy or sad? Do they look deep in thought or without a care in the world? They might be looking peaceful or full of life.

Position a child so that their back is turned to the painting, and teach them how to hold the mirror so that they can see the picture behind them and their face at the same time. You will need to guide them until they have got the mirror in the right position. Now ask the child if they can replicate the expression of the person in the picture. It helps if the picture chosen has someone with a clear emotional expression.

Encourage the child to look at the overall pose of the portrait's subject and to mimic that as well. How does it make the child feel? Do they feel strong and powerful or quiet and subdued? This additional element of the activity provides a good opportunity for discussing what it must be like to sit for a portrait for hours at a time.

When the final expression and pose have been struck, take a photo so that a display can be made back at the setting to remind the children of the painting.

After the visit

Tissue paper explorations

You will need:

- A reproduction of a painting which shows a wide range of colours

- Clear acetate (OHP paper or clear plastic squares – big rolls of OHP paper can be obtained from most hardware stores)

- A quantity of tissue paper in a variety of colours (cheaper tissue paper bleeds more when moistened, which can be better for this activity)

- Big brushes or sponges

- Diluted PVA glue

This is a great activity for looking at and responding to colours that may have been a focus during the gallery visit. The process for the children is enjoyable and allows them to work independently, and the final effect is very rewarding, especially when viewed next to a window or over a light-box. Tissue paper has such rich sensory qualities. The sound of it scrunching, the way the colour changes when it is held up to different lights and shadows and the tactile sensation of tearing the paper lead to creative learning experiences.

- Display the reproduction of the picture so that the children can look at the colours within it.

- Spread the diluted glue on to the plastic sheeting. (The children can either do this individually or as a collaborative activity.)

- Tear up pieces of the tissue paper and look carefully again at the way the colour is used in the reproduction of the painting.

- Cover the surface of the plastic with the tissue shapes, overlapping and piecing the shapes together like a jigsaw. Refer again to the reproduction of the painting and try to represent how the colours are used in it.

- Add one more layer of glue on the top to stick the tissue paper together and to add a sheen.

- Once dry, carefully peel the tissue paper off the plastic. You'll find that the plastic sheet will show the colours of the tissue paper shapes.

- You can display the plastic sheet or the tissue paper sheet next to the reproduction of the painting to draw attention to the painting's use of colour.

Role-play art shop

Turn your role-play area into an art shop selling a range of materials and including a demonstration space. This area can be a useful mark-making area for emergent writing skills. All your baskets of pencils, felt-tip pens, charcoal, chalk, etc. can be stored in this role-play area. Include a variety of paper for mark-making. You could also set up an area for testing out the materials.

Art gallery role-play

You can also transform an area of your setting into an art gallery. Case study 7 describes how this encouraged the children to re-enact their recent visit to a local gallery.

Case Study 7

Art gallery role-play

Somerset House Nursery School, London

This case study describes an enjoyable role-play activity which followed a group of children's visit to their local art gallery.

Somerset House Nursery School arranges frequent visits to local art galleries. When the children visit a gallery (with a one to two adult:child ratio) they travel on a bus and take a packed lunch with them. They find somewhere to eat it on the grass nearby, and then visit the art gallery.

After the visit, the children re-enact what happened. Gallery role-play in the setting begins with the children taking the bus and pretending to eat their packed lunch. This is to help recall and familiarization.

The role-play includes a staffed ticket office and gallery guides, with all roles taken by the children. Working from a reproduction, the children dress up a child in similar clothes to a person from a painting. The child then poses next to the painting so that the other children can make comparisons. This is effective even for the 3 and 4-year-olds.

Talented parents and carers come in and paint. The smells of oil and pastels are evocative and contribute to the effectiveness of the role-play. Following a theme, such as portraits or flowers, the children draw or paint pictures and stick them on the wall among famous reproductions. The children take it very seriously, and spend time flicking through the art books provided in the role-play area. They talk about the paintings and take other children around the space, role-playing a tour guide.

Aspects of this role-play can take place before the visit, which can help model behaviour for the actual visit.

Working art studio

An inspiring learning opportunity for the Early Years setting is to establish an art studio. In an art studio, children can return to and continue with their art creations rather than have to complete their work in one session. By returning to their work, they have time to reflect and respond to their own and their friends' discoveries and achievements. This may not be something the children are used to, but the studio will nurture learning skills of this kind, where the process is the driving force rather than the end product. This is also an important factor when encouraging children to define their own artistic styles over a long period.

Some useful organizational starting points are:

- Identify a corner within your setting that has enough floor and wall space for a studio. This will depend on the size of the setting as a whole, but flexibility is crucial so that the space can be extended and reduced in size where necessary.

- Attach paper to the wall, vertically and horizontally, on which the children can draw or paint. The paper can be attached to an easel instead, but it's advantageous to use the wall because work can be left on display in an unfinished state more easily, and the wall space can accommodate more of the children's work.

- Create a washing line of work. This can be strung up for drying out or storing unfinished work, and adds a lovely 'working' element to the studio space. (Sensors in settings can sometimes be a problem, but this can be solved by hanging the string low and by finding areas which cannot be detected!)

- Provide accessible materials. This is perhaps the most important feature of an art studio, because the space should promote independent and child-initiated learning as much as possible. Paints, charcoal, pencils, graphite pencils, tissue paper pieces, glue, felt-tip pens, etc. must be clearly accessible to the children at all times so they can select the materials for themselves.

- Provide light-boxes to encourage exploration of colour, and mirrors to extend work with light and shadow.

- Create portfolios. As the work in the studio accumulates, the results can be stored in whole class portfolios or individual folders, but these should still be accessible for the children to review and consult.

- Use card samples of paint colours from decorating shops. These can inspire exploration of colour.

- Display artwork. You can enhance the atmosphere of the studio by adding artefacts and reproductions of famous artwork, perhaps connected to a gallery visit made earlier. Intersperse these with the children's work.

Case Study 8

Art studio

Parklands Early Years Centre, Leeds

Staff from Parklands Early Years Centre have created a room within their setting especially for creative activities. This works extremely well because of the way the room is designed. It is completely empty so that nothing diverts the children's attention away from the activities on offer. The flooring is vinyl and there is a large notice board on one wall. Blackout blinds and dimmer light switches can create a completely dark space, and art activities have included the use of torches and overhead projectors to take full advantage of this.

The centre ran art-related activities in the space for 13 weeks in partnership with resident artists. The theme for the project was 'Where things come from and where things go'. Each week photographs of the previous week's activities were displayed on the notice board to remind the children of their past work. As the work accumulated, the story of the children's artistic journeys evolved. A visit to Leeds City Art Gallery formed part of the 13-week programme for some of the children taking part.

Sample art session

Activities were run in the room for six children at a time with accompanying key workers. Four sessions were run each day, involving 24 children in total. In the first week the session focused on ice, which was provided in different shapes and colours. Some ice blocks contained natural objects inside them. The children could explore the material at their own pace using a range of different approaches. For example, coloured ice was melted on to large sheets of paper, mixed in with other coloured ice and swirled around. There were no 'rules' and children were encouraged to be freely expressive. The ice could be smashed up by them and played with in any ways they wanted.

Benefits

The art space provided the children with an environment away from all the distractions of their usual setting. The children behaved differently in the art space as a result. It was liberating and unusual for them to play in a space where there were no rules. The children benefited enormously from the focused creative work which took place regularly over a sustained period. Evaluation revealed a defined improvement in the children's language, confidence and involvement. The children also became increasingly skilful at producing original ideas and in developing them as the sessions unfolded.

Other ideas for continual work

Using paintings as a learning resource

It is well worth investing in a book that is rich in reproductions of paintings. You can look at this whenever you are planning a new topic. For example, if you are exploring buildings as a topic, find paintings that show different buildings in various environments. For inner-city settings, paintings showing beach scenes and the countryside in evocative ways will be of great interest to the children. Paintings can also provide excellent visual references when investigating colours or shapes.

Exposing children to works of art in the setting

Most Early Years settings are visually stimulating environments, with colourful displays and plenty of books. It's easy to include within this environment reproductions of works of art, whether they have been cut from magazines, bought from your local art gallery or ordered from an educational catalogue. Books showing works of art can also be bought for the children to look through along with the other books provided. You will find that these additions provide a rich resource leading to questioning and discussion.

Observational artwork

You can encourage children to draw or paint from observation by providing attractive opportunities within the setting. You can set up a 'still life' corner, where children take it in turns each week to bring in an object of their choice. An easel and varied art materials will provide further incentives. Weekly displays can show the range of interpretations that result when one object is drawn or painted by different children, and comparing these interpretations can stimulate interesting discussions. All of these suggested components of observational drawing will result in the children becoming more discerning about works of art and art in general.

Curriculum Links

1. Art I Spy
2. What's in the picture?
3. Noisy pictures
4. Drawing
5. Pipe-cleaner poses
6. Treasure hunt
7. Colour quest
8. Mirror mimicking
9. Tissue paper explorations
10. Role-play art shop
11. Art gallery role-play
12. Working art studio

Early Learning Goals	Activity	Area of Learning
Continue to be interested, excited and motivated to learn.	All	PSE: Dispositions and attitudes
Be confident to try out new activities, indicate ideas and speak in a familiar group.	1, 2, 3, 10, 11, 12	
Maintain attention, concentrate, and sit quietly when appropriate.	1, 2	
Respond to significant experiences, showing a range of feelings when appropriate.	3, 8, 10, 11, 12	PSE: Self-confidence and self-control
Have a developing awareness of their own needs, views and feelings and be sensitive to the needs, views and feelings of others.	2, 3, 10, 11, 12	
Have a developing respect for their own cultures and beliefs and those of others.	8	
Work as part of a group or class, taking turns and sharing fairly, understanding that there needs to be agreed values and codes of behaviour for groups of people, including adults and children, to work together harmoniously.	2, 3, 10, 11, 12	PSE: Making relationships
Understand what is right and what is wrong.	3	PSE: Self behaviour and self-control
Consider the consequences of their words and actions for themselves and others.	10, 11, 12	
Select and use activities and resources independently.	5, 10, 11, 12	PSE: Self-care

▶

Early Learning Goals	Activity	Area of Learning
Understand that people have different needs, views, cultures and beliefs, that need to be treated with respect.	10, 11, 12	PSE: Sense of community
Interact with others, negotiating plans and activities and taking turns in conversation.	1, 2	CLL: Language for communication
Enjoy listening to and using spoken and written language, and readily turn to it in their play and learning.	10, 11, 12	
Sustain attentive listening, responding to what they have heard by relevant comments, questions or actions.	1, 2	
Extend their vocabulary, exploring the meanings and sounds of new words.	1, 2, 6, 7	
Speak clearly and audibly with confidence and control and show awareness of the listener, for example by their use of conventions such as greetings, 'please' and 'thank you'.	6, 7	
Use language to imagine and recreate roles and experiences.	3, 6, 7, 10, 11, 12	CLL: Language for thinking
Use talk to organize, sequence and clarify thinking, ideas, feelings and events.	6	
Attempt writing for different purposes, using features of different forms such as lists, stories and instructions.	10, 11, 12	CLL: Writing
Write their own names and other things such as labels and captions and begin to form simple sentences, sometimes using punctuation.	10, 11, 12	
Use developing mathematical ideas and methods to solve practical problems.	10, 11, 12	MD: Numbers as labels and for counting
Talk about and recognize and recreate simple patterns.	1, 2	MD: Shape and space
Use language such as 'circle', 'bigger' to describe the shape and size of solids and flat shapes.	1, 9	
Use everyday words to describe position.	2, 9, 10, 11, 12	
Investigate objects and materials by using all their senses as appropriate.	3, 4, 6, 7, 8	KNU: Exploration and investigation
Find out more about and identify some features of living things, objects and events they observe.	1, 2, 6, 7, 8	
Look closely at similarities, differences, patterns and change.	1, 2	
Build and construct with a wide range of objects, selecting appropriate resources and adapting their work where necessary.	5, 10, 11, 12	KNU: Designing and making skills
Select the tools and techniques they need to shape, assemble and join materials they are using.	9, 10, 11, 12	

Early Learning Goals	Activity	Area of Learning
Find out about and identify the uses of everyday technology and use information and communication technology and programmable toys to support their learning.	10, 11, 12	KNU: Information and communication technology
Find out about past and present events in their own lives, and those of their families and other people they know.	8, 10, 11, 12	KNU: Sense of time
Observe, find out about and identify features in the place they live and the natural world.	2, 3, 6, 7	KNU: Sense of place
Begin to know about their own cultures and beliefs and those of other people.	8, 10, 11, 12	KNU: Cultures and beliefs
Use a range of small and large equipment.	5, 9, 10, 11, 12	PD: Using equipment
Handle tools, objects, construction and malleable materials safely and with increasing control.	9, 10, 11, 12	PD: Using tools and materials
Explore colour, texture, shape, form, space in two or three dimensions.	1, 2, 5, 6, 7, 8, 9, 10, 11, 12	CD: Exploring media and materials
Use their imagination in art and design, music, dance, imaginative and role play and stories.	8, 9, 10, 11, 12	CD: Imagination
Respond in a variety of ways to what they see, hear, smell, touch and feel. Express and communicate their ideas, thoughts and feelings by using a widening range of materials, suitable tools, imaginative and role play, movement, designing and making and a variety of songs and musical instruments.	3, 5, 9 5, 6, 7, 9, 10, 11, 12	CD: Responding to experiences, and expressing and communicating ideas

CHAPTER 3

The Performing Arts

This chapter is divided into the following sections:

- How the performing arts can help young children learn

- Dance and movement

- Music

- Drama and mime

- Puppetry

This chapter suggests different activities you can do in your setting either before or after a visit to a performance. The activities can serve as preparation for the performance, or as follow-up ideas to sustain the experience. If you use the activities after the visit to the performing arts venue, you can build in ideas, characters and themes from the performance itself.

How the performing arts can help young children learn

Attending a performance can be very exciting for young children. There is always a sense of anticipation as the lights dim and the children realize their role as spectators. Activities in the setting either before or after a performance can be participative, encouraging children to be performers themselves. There are numerous benefits to be gained from the performing arts, either through attending performances or by participating. The list below highlights some of these.

Attending or participating in performance arts:

- Encourages children's creativity

- Raises children's self-esteem

- Enhances children's learning through the act of participation

- Develops children's communication skills

- Encourages children's freedom of expression and individuality

- Stimulates children who have different learning styles

- Provides extended opportunities for cross-curricular learning

- Provides rich resources through which different cultures can be explored

Dance and movement

Movement comes naturally to everyone. As children get older, movement can develop into dancing, which is especially enjoyed when accompanied by music. Dancing develops children's sense of rhythm, which can in turn contribute to linguistic development. Dancing also clearly benefits physical health and well-being, and can be encouraged for that reason alone.

These activities are suitable for both before and after the children have attended a dance performance. If you are initiating the activities after the visit, you can adapt them to suit the themes and characters featured in the performance.

Busy beans warm-up activity

You will need a space large enough for children to move around quickly and safely. Ask the children to move around the space, being careful not to collide with others. Call out the bean names, to which the children can respond physically according to the following directions:

- *Chili beans*: shiver/shake as if you are very cold.

- *Runner beans*: run quickly on the spot.

- *Jumping beans*: bounce on the move or on the spot.

- *Baked beans*: fall slowly to the floor as if you're melting.

- *Jelly beans*: wobble on the spot.

- *Broad beans*: make a wide shape.

Musical statues

Musical statues can be used as a warm-up for dance activities, or it can stand alone as an exploration of movements and shapes.

The aim of the game is to keep as still as possible when the music stops playing. The child showing the most movement while trying to keep still sits down, and the game continues until only one child is left standing up. It's important to keep the atmosphere light and jokey while playing this game, so that it doesn't become too competitive.

Variations

- Children can dance in pairs holding one or both hands, which makes it all the more difficult to keep still when the music stops.

- When the music stops, children can freeze in the shape of an object, such as a pencil, a tree, or a cat – whatever they or you choose.

- You can explore gesture, developing the 'freeze' idea suggested above to include feelings. This is effective with older children, especially if you are exploring feelings as a topic. You can ask the children to respond like a statue expressing an emotion such as 'excited', 'angry', 'happy' or 'lonely' when the music stops.

Animal movements

This movement and dance activity works well if you use illustrated story books about animals as a starting point. Illustrations in big books are ideal for this as they can be shared by a group.

The movement should take place in a big space, standing up. The responses from the children will be more creative if they are standing, rather than sitting, as you read through the story together.

- Talk about an animal's features with the children using a large illustrated book. If the animal has paws, ask them how it might use them, such as for washing or digging. If it's a bird, you can talk about how its wings are outstretched when flying. If it's an animal which lives in water, you can discuss how it might move underwater or swim at the water's surface. Ask how the animal might eat, sleep, or move when it's frightened or tired.

- Children can come up with movements for all of the characteristics discussed and everyone can copy those suggested.

- Let the children explore all or any of the movements at their own pace. If you think that a more structured approach would be useful, take them through the different ideas for movement one by one.

Variations

- This activity can be developed into a dance either with or without music. You can try it both ways. Music makes the activity more fun and encourages more movements.

- When you and the children become familiar with this activity you can play with the order of the movements and the pace at which they are danced.

- You can also encourage children to dance with a partner, each doing their own animal movements.

Dance and movement

Sticky Fingers Playgroup, Caehopkins School, Powys

Sticky Fingers Playgroup invited dance organization Powys Dance to perform their show called **The Present** to the playgroup's 30 children aged between 2 and 6 years old. Powys Dance ran two INSET sessions for Early Years practitioners before the performance. This enabled the staff at the setting to conduct dance and movement activities with the children before they saw the performance. The activities also familiarized the children with the main themes, which explored the movements of bears, birds and monkeys.

The children loved watching the performance and the setting has continued to run dance activities for half an hour each week. Activities have included exploring dance movements to accompany well-known nursery rhymes and a story about going on safari. The children made clothes and jewellery to wear, and split into two groups to perform their pieces to each other.

The children have benefited from continual dance activity. The staff at the setting had identified dance as a gap in the children's everyday experiences, and now see the children increasingly able to express themselves in different ways. The children are also exposed to different cultures and music through the activities, and are skilful at responding to different music through their own interpretations.

If the children have attended a dance performance earlier, you can adapt the activities suggested above to remind the children of it. You can talk with the children about the themes which were in the dance, and they can remind each other of the characters featured. Were there particular ways in which the characters moved? Children could copy distinctive movements they remember. Was there a favourite part of the performance for the children? Key elements can be picked out and developed. For example, if there was a part where a character tumbled on to the ground, you could explore the physical movements of tumbling, rolling and twisting. If a character crouched low or reached high, you could all experiment with these moves. Music will stimulate the children to explore these physical movements freely and at their own pace.

Music

An appreciation of music relies on listening and not watching. Music therefore contributes in a very pleasurable way to the development of listening skills. It can be just as expressive as dance, as dramatic as theatre and as captivating as puppetry, but its impact is heard and not seen. However, when music is linked to dance, theatre and puppetry, a visual element accompanies the sounds. This can be very helpful in building young children's musical appreciation. Components of music include rhythm, pitch and volume, among others. Investigating all of these can contribute to children's linguistic development, and can provide a basis for enjoyable activities.

A steady beat

The following activity has been reproduced from the First Notes Resource Pack, with kind permission from soundLINCS, Lincolnshire Music Development Agency.

- Stand the children in a circle.

- Establish a steady beat (pulse) by clapping until everyone is clapping together.

- Vary the speed of the pulse (or the tempo) so that the clapping is faster or slower.

- Once the children seem confident with maintaining a steady pulse, use percussion instruments or dowel sticks instead of clapping.

- Try to 'pass' a pulse around the circle instead of everyone playing together.

Variation

- Make a jingle rope with the children before the activity. This involves stringing penne pasta, bells and big beads on to individual pieces of string so that there are many short ropes. These are then tied together to form a large jingle rope like a giant necklace, which can be held collectively by all the participating children. The children can shake the jingle rope in a circle to the rhythm. (The jingle rope can then be used for different sound exercises in other activities.)

Soundscape: what's the weather?

Creating a soundscape is a way of painting a picture through sound. The 'picture' can be of any-thing – a railway station, a day at the seaside, or a traffic jam on a busy street. Building a picture of rapidly changing weather conditions is an effective way of introducing children to creating pictures through the world of sound.

You can include some simple instruments for this activity, although it also works well using hands and bodies to create sounds. If you choose to use instruments, you can make your own using empty plastic containers. Fill them half-way with pulses or rice and seal the top with paper and a strong elastic band. It's wise to limit the use of instruments, homemade or otherwise, to just two or three, because they can cause the body sounds to be less audible and less effective.

Soundscape activities are more successful if you can build a sense of expectation and excitement beforehand.

- Gather the children together and ask them if they can help make a picture using sounds. Explain that together you will be thinking of the best sounds to represent different weather conditions. These can be as imaginative as you wish.

- The different ways the body can make sounds can be discussed and tried out with the children. Some of these are:
  - clapping hands
  - tapping two fingers from one hand on to two fingers of the other
  - patting thighs
  - rubbing the palms of the hands together

- clicking the fingers (some children find this difficult)
- tapping feet on the floor
- stamping the feet on the floor
- making a clicking sound with the tongue.

■ Together, work out sounds to represent different kinds of weather. The different weather types could be:
- the sun shining out from a cloud
- light rain, pitter-pattering
- heavy rain, drumming on to the ground
- snow softly falling
- hailstones hitting the ground and bouncing back up again
- a blazing hot day without a cloud in the sky.

■ Start with an easy example, like rain. Decide which sounds, and/or instruments, best describe different types of rain.

■ Simple role-play of looking up at the sun coming out of the clouds might prompt a child to suggest an accompanying sound, for example the shimmer of a tambourine or the rubbing together of palms.

■ Now link the sounds together through speaking the different weather types out loud like a story. *The day started beautifully. The sun came out from behind a cloud and shone on everyone below.* (Leave a pause for the children to make the agreed 'sun' sound.) *But then, a drop of water came down from the sky. Then another, and another … etc.*

■ You can develop this idea of narrative by introducing events into the story, for example children running out to play and splashing in the puddles, or a horse clip-clopping along the road.

■ Case Study 10 suggests an effective addition to this activity.

■ To add a sense of occasion to the activity, the group of children could perform their soundscape to other children at your setting.

Case Study 10

Forte and piano (Loud and quiet) – LSO Discovery

The London Symphony Orchestra runs a programme for young children called Discovery, which is funded by Youth Music and Sure Start Islington South. This activity explores the musical concepts of quiet (**piano**, in Italian) and loud (**forte**), which can be used in the setting. The setting's practitioner 'conducting' the proceedings will help children understand the role of the conductor of an orchestra, as well as encouraging them to follow the activity carefully.

Case Study 10 *continued*

To make some gentle rain music:

- Ask everyone to drum their fingers very quietly on the tabletop.

- Now make it pour with rain. Everyone bangs their hands rapidly on the table (or if you prefer, on their knees).

- Devise two signals, one to represent quiet rain and the other to represent a downpour.

- With you as conductor, practise raining **piano**, then immediately **forte**, then **piano** again until everyone responds immediately to your signals.

High and low

The following activity has been reproduced from the First Notes Resource Pack, with kind permission from soundLINCS, Lincolnshire Music Development Agency.

- Choose a high sound and a low sound (these can be played on a chime bar or keyboard instrument, for example).

- Ask the children to reach up tall when you play the high sound, and touch the floor when you play the low sound.

- Vary the order in which you play the sounds and encourage the children to move according to what they hear.

- Children can take turns to lead the activity by playing the sounds to which the rest of the group move.

Variation

- Children move to the sounds and freeze as statues when you stop playing (like musical statues). If the last sound you played was a high sound, they should make a tall statue, and if the last sound was a low one, they should make a low statue. Children could suggest a 'middle' pose to represent a sound played between the high sound and the low sound.

Developing an appreciation of music

Appreciating the components of music illustrated through the activities provided here will help the children when they go to a concert. You will need to find performances which are tailored to the children's age range, as the standard length of concerts will be too long for sustained listening. (Some organizations that provide information about concerts for the Early Years are listed in Further Information at the back of this book.) During the performance the children are likely to have to sit quietly while listening. However, you can explore children's physical and emotional responses to the music after returning from the concert to the setting. Children will often have views on whether they liked the music and if it reminded them of other music they have heard.

You can include music appreciation into the daily activities at your setting. One way of doing this is to play a few minutes of a piece of recorded music following circle time, letting children move to the music however they wish. Encourage the children to bring in a piece of music of their choice when they have become familiar with this routine. Try to ensure that the children listen to a range of musical styles. For example, if the children have chosen mostly popular music, you could provide a short classical piece when it is your turn to play music. The daily routine of listening to music will be useful when you have a visit planned to a concert hall. You can introduce relevant music and talk about the instruments in the week leading up to the visit, so that the children become increasingly familiar with the music they will be listening to during the performance.

Drama and mime

Children's participation in drama activities builds their self-confidence, and gives them opportunities for self-expression in a safe and playful environment. There are many ways this can be brought about in your setting through simple play-based activities. The activities suggested below can be explored before going to the theatre to familiarize children with the principles of drama. The themes and characters introduced during the performance can be followed up afterwards. Further ideas for sustaining the experience of going to the theatre are given on pages 46 and 47.

Let's pretend

Children love pretending, and need little encouragement to enact emotions and narratives. Drama and mime can be more effective when time has been set aside especially for these activities. To ritualize creative drama-based activities, you can define a circle or square with tape, inside which only acting or pretending can take place. Another such technique is starting and ending the pretending session with everyone spinning on the spot. The spin at the beginning of the session represents a move into the make-believe world, and the spin at the end returns the children back to reality.

The following two activities for this section have been inspired by ideas generously provided by the Half Moon Young People's Theatre.

Magic watering can

You can start this activity by using a real watering can, but as the children become more familiar with it an imaginary watering can is equally effective. The watering can transforms anything or anyone 'splashed' by the water. The water is imaginary, of course, but you can use pieces of silk to flow out of the watering can, if you wish. This excites positive responses from the children as it touches them.

Start with everyone sitting in a circle. Explain that everyone will change when the watering can splashes them, and choose the things the children will become, for example a dog, a cat, a tree swaying in the wind, a bubbling soup on the hob, a witch, etc. Ritualize each role by asking everyone to curl up on the floor. Count up to three before saying the character the children will become: '1, 2, 3 … we're all going to be dogs'. Move around the circle, splashing the children in turn, allowing them free rein in their interpretation of their roles. Each child can then have a turn at walking around the circle, splashing the group and choosing how everyone will transform.

This activity can work equally well using imaginary magic paint, powder or moon-dust.

3.1 Tiger Story, Our Lady and St Anne's Roman Catholic Primary School

What's on the floor?

Encourage the children to spin on the spot to indicate that they are now in the world of pretending. Introduce the activity, counting '1, 2, 3 …' followed by telling the children the type of ground they are walking on. The ground can be spiky, slippery, hot, bouncy, sticky, etc. Let everyone have a go at saying what the ground is like.

Older children enjoy exploring emotions in this activity. The ground can make the children 'angry', prompting some very cross body language from children as they stomp around the space with hunched shoulders. The ground can also make the children 'happy', or 'shy', and so on.

Copycats

This activity can be as simple or as complex as you like, depending on the children's responses. The children need to be in pairs. They take it in turns to lead the activity, which involves one child doing a simple action and the other child copying it.

- The two children stand face to face. The first child thinks of a simple action, like eating a piece of cake or ironing, and their partner copies it. This mime can be repeated at least once so that the partner can copy it as exactly as possible.

- The children can then swap roles so that the partner is now the 'leader' of the duo.

- This idea can be developed so that the 'leader' shows an action quite slowly and the partner mimes that action as simultaneously as possible. Children may understand this immediately if you liken the partner to a 'mirror' for the leader.

- Some children may like to invent their own actions, but others may prefer to have actions suggested to them.

Case Study 11

Mary Sambrook Children's Centre and the Half Moon Young People's Theatre

Staff from the Half Moon Young People's Theatre in London worked with practitioners and children from the Mary Sambrook Children's Centre before and after the children attended the performance **Grubs, Slugs and Boogie Bugs**. In this case study, the setting's manager describes how the experience, funded by Sure Start Tower Hamlets, has become integrated into the children's learning on a daily basis.

Three practitioners from the setting attended training sessions before the staff from the Half Moon Theatre visited us. We were introduced to the activities the children would be undertaking, which was very useful for us for when we in turn worked with the setting's children using creative drama techniques. After the staff from Half Moon Theatre had visited us twice, we were confident enough to run activities with the children on our own, integrating the drama techniques into circle time regularly. There are strategies which we learnt, such as clapping to signify when an activity was to start or finish. These strategies introduced boundaries for the children, providing for them the space in which to be creative.

The age of our children ranges from 18 months to 5 years old. We do a lot of creative work at the setting, but running consistent drama activities has definitely developed the children's creativity and self-esteem. It's also given the staff the confidence to try out their own ideas and to encourage the children to do the same. The workshops with Half Moon Theatre were very tactile and multi-sensory, which is very important for our children with special needs. Parents have become involved too, with some attending all of the four workshops.

Using existing stories or nursery rhymes

The activities described above provide a good introduction to enacting children's favourite stories from books. Case Study 12 describes how Humpty Dumpty is brought to life by using drama and role-play. You can introduce props if you wish, although this is not necessary. Imaginary cups and saucers at a tea party are as effective as the real items.

Case Study 12

Humpty Dumpty

This activity was developed for young children by the theatre company Arts On The Move, and illustrates how you can use a well-known nursery rhyme or story to explore techniques of drama.

Ask the children to recite the nursery rhyme with you:

> Humpty Dumpty sat on a wall
>
> Humpty Dumpty had a great fall
>
> All the King's horses and all the King's men
>
> Couldn't put Humpty together again

Now add movements and ask the children to act out the movements with you:

Humpty Dumpty sat on a wall

'Let's sit on our wall — ooh! It's a bit high!'
Pretend to be sitting on a high wall. Look down and show how frightened you are about being so high up.

Humpty Dumpty had a great fall

Fall on to the floor. Carefully!

All the King's horses and all the King's men

Stand up quickly. Pretend to be riding a horse. Sit up straight to show that you're important.

Couldn't put Humpty together again

Stand looking down at Humpty, scratching your head.
Look at each other — 'I don't think we can mend him.'

The activity goes on to describe how the situation presented in the nursery rhyme can be resolved through various decisions and actions, such as mending the broken eggshell, making the wall shorter, and making the surface of the ground softer. These ideas can be suggested and acted out by the children.

Post-performance activities

Explorations of themes

You can take any small element of a performance and develop it as a drama or mime activity with the children. A tea party featured in the performance can be developed into a full-scale celebration. Weather can also be explored. For example, if it had snowed in the play's story, you could all role-play being outside in the snow, feeling the snow falling on your faces, playing with snowballs, stomping in the snow, shivering and building snow-people. Encourage the children to come up with their own ideas for the role-play, with everyone acting them out.

Discussion

Theatrical performances often explore the feelings of the featured characters. Use this as an opportunity to explore feelings in general, and those specific to the play. How would the children themselves feel if they were in that situation? Would they have responded in the same way as the characters did?

Art responses

You can recapture the magic of the performance by providing art activities which are accessible and which encourage children to respond immediately. The children can explore characters through drawing and model-making, or they can explore concepts and themes through abstract means. The activity below describes how children can create abstract artwork and soundscapes after watching a performance.

Collaborative art reflections

You will need:

- A wide range of mark-making materials: chalk, charcoal, pastels, crayons, felt-tip pens, etc.

- Large pieces of paper, for example A1 size.

Create a big space where the paper can be put down with the materials laid out for all to use. Encourage the children to draw and make marks in response to the performance they have just seen. If it had a definite story you could talk this through together as a reminder, either as they are drawing or before. Children may wish to focus on a particular theme or character through their artwork. Make sure this activity is large-scale and collaborative, so the children see and respond to each other's interpretations as the activity is taking place. If you can find suitable music which reflects the performance, play this while the children are pursuing the art activity.

Puppetry

Puppet shows are usually story-based, offering rich opportunities for creative activities after the experience. Children can develop characters presented in the story through extended artwork, re-enactment and their own use of puppets, if they are available. Operating a puppet as a speaker can help children lose their inhibitions, and can raise their self-esteem and build self-confidence. Using puppets encourages and develops the social and personal skills needed for early language development. Puppet performances can be played out individually or in small and large groups, where children can learn to listen to and respond to one another.

You can sustain the children's interest by using puppets in your setting on a regular basis. If you can obtain examples of different types of puppets, you can use circle time to examine puppets from around the world. You can encourage the children to work the puppets, and enhance the sense of occasion by filming what they do.

Puppets exist in many forms, but the most common types might include:

- Hand or glove puppets

- Rod puppets (including shadow puppets)

- Marionette or string puppets

Making puppets

Build puppetry into any topic you may be working on. If you are investigating 'animals', or 'myself', for example, you can include a puppet-making activity. The simplest puppets made from a sock or a spoon leads to imaginative areas of learning.

Painted hands and fingers

You will need:

- Hands, fingers, feet and toes

- Finger paints, face paints in a variety of colours

- Water-based, non-toxic pens

- Body glitter

- Warm water, sponge and soap

Using face paints and body paints and glitter, draw faces and expressions on the back or the palm of hands. You could paint the fingers as hair and the thumb as the nose so that when held up, palm facing out, the hand looks like the side profile of a comical face. Drawing an eye on the back of the hand will enhance this effect. Creasing hands up and wiggling the fingers breathes life into the puppet as the 'face' moves and makes different expressions. Children can also paint their toes to make puppets.

Case Study 13

Wooden spoon puppets

Discover, East London

Discover is a creative learning space for children aged up to 8 years old and their parents, carers and teachers. This case study shows how simple, everyday materials can motivate young children to create new characters and stories.

During a visit to Discover, the children are encouraged to create different characters using a variety of imaginative methods. All visiting children are given a small wooden spoon, together with a selection of fabrics, paper scraps, pipe-cleaners, scissors and masking tape. The children dress their spoons with the materials provided, draw on facial characteristics and add arms using the pipe-cleaners. Children will often spend up to 20 minutes creating their puppet, and will give their character a name and a place to live.

Case Study *continued*

A special puppet theatre at Discover motivates the children to use their spoon puppets to create stories. This is continued at their setting through role-play and puppet shows. Practitioners have commented on how the children's language and storytelling skills have developed by using the spoon puppets as character props during their play.

Character gloves

You will need:

- A variety of gloves: rubber, surgical, woollen, cloth, etc.
- Odds and ends for decoration: buttons, toy eyes, wool, fabric, etc.
- PVA glue and plastic spreaders
- Scissors

Children can select their own materials from the resources provided to make each finger of their glove a different character. If the children have attended a puppet performance, the characters can be inspired by those featured in the show, or new characters can be created.

Photograph puppets

You will need:

- A camera and film or digital camera
- Printed photographs
- Card
- Glue and scissors
- Lollypop sticks
- Masking tape

Children can take digital photographs of each other in dressing-up clothes related to the puppet performance they have attended. The photographs can then be printed out. Cut around the outline of the posing child on the photograph and mount the cut-out on to card. Stick lollypop sticks on the back of the cut-out with tape to create a set of puppets which can be brought to life with a table-top puppet theatre.

Some simple-to-make puppet theatres

If you can include a simple puppet theatre in your setting, children will be naturally drawn to perform and play with their puppets. Place a mirror a metre or so in front of any of the theatres listed below so that the children can see their own performance.

Table theatre

- Lay a big cloth over a table making sure that there is an opening at the front drop of the cloth.

- The children position themselves under the table with the cloth covering everything but their hands, so that the puppets can stick out to perform for the audience.

Upside-down theatre

- Turn a table upside down so that the legs stick upwards.

- Attach a cloth or a sheet of paper large enough to wrap around the two table legs facing the audience.

- The children can hide themselves behind this screen and show only their puppets performing above the top of it.

3.2 Shadow Puppetry, St Werburghs Park Nursery School

The doorway

- Staple a piece of white cloth across the lower half of a doorway. For reasons of safety, the doorway to be used needs to be in an undisturbed area of your setting, for example it could be the doorway of a walk-in cupboard used to store resources.

- You can shine a light source behind the cloth just behind the children operating their puppets to create shadows. If you are using a resource cupboard, for example, the light source will be set up in the cupboard, and the children will also be positioned in the cupboard.

Some examples of how to use shadows in puppetry are described in Case Study 14.

Case Study 14

Exploring shadows and projected images
St Werburghs Park Nursery School, Bristol

Shadow puppeteer Richard Hughes worked with children from St Werburghs Park Nursery School in Bristol, developing with them the areas of role-play, puppetry and storytelling. The project was funded by the Arts Council of England. Small and large groups of children were involved in a range of activities, which ran two days a week for six weeks. These included investigating the concepts of light and shade, drawing, working with different materials to produce different effects, and using narrative to create stories. The project was run flexibly so that it could respond continually to the ideas of the participating children. Richard Hughes describes how he worked creatively with the children, experimenting with shapes and light to produce shadows and stories.

My work with the children began with questions:

- What is a shadow?
- Where/when can we see shadows?
- Whose shadow is that?
- How can you tell?
- How can we make our shadows bigger or smaller?
- What would happen if ...?
- What other ways can we make shadows?

We found objects and toys from the group's setting which made interesting shadow images. We started to play with two or more shadows combining them to create new images and to develop dialogue and role-play. Then we started to make specific images to support a train of thought, for example, what the pirates could do with a boat. I asked, 'How can we make a shadow that looks like a ship?'

The project sparked the children's imaginations in new ways and introduced them to new creative media. The setting's practitioner has noticed a difference in the nature of the children's play since the visit. For example, the boys in the setting enjoy Power Ranger role-play. This has now become less aggressive and more creative.

The chairs

- Place two chairs so that the seats of the chairs are facing each other (i.e. not back to back).

- Position the chairs so that they are about a metre apart from each other.

- Lay a pole between the two chairs so that the ends rest on the chair seats, and fix the ends with string or tape so that the pole remains firm.

- Drape a cloth over the pole. This is the screen of the theatre. The children can hide behind the screen and show only their puppets performing above the top of it.

The window

- On a clear day, move puppets up and down on a ground floor window ledge to create a performance for the audience.

- Children can either position themselves outdoors, performing to an audience sitting indoors, or vice versa.

Curriculum Links

1. Busy beans

2. Musical statues

3. Animal movements

4. A steady beat

5. Soundscape

6. High and low

7. Let's pretend:
   - Magic watering can
   - What's on the floor?
   - Copycats

8. Using stories and rhymes

9. Collaborative art reflections

10. Puppets

Early Learning Goals	Activity	Area of Learning
Continue to be interested, excited and motivated to learn.	All	PSE: Dispositions and attitudes
Be confident to try out new activities, indicate ideas and speak in a familiar group.	3, 4, 7, 10	
Maintain attention, concentrate, and sit quietly when appropriate.	2	
Respond to significant experiences, showing a range of feelings when appropriate.	6	PSE: Self-confidence and self-esteem
Have a developing awareness of their own needs, views and feelings and be sensitive to the needs, views and feelings of others.	4, 7	
Form good relationships with adults and peers.	2,7	PSE: Making relationships
Work as part of a group or class, taking turns and sharing fairly, understanding that there needs to be agreed values and codes of behaviour for groups of people, including adults and children, to work together harmoniously	2, 4, 5, 7, 8, 10	
Select and use activities and resources independently.	7	PSE: Self-care
Understand that people have different needs, views, cultures and beliefs, that need to be treated with respect.	5, 7	PSE: Sense of community
Understand that they can expect others to treat their needs, views, cultures and beliefs with respect.	5, 7	
Interact with others, negotiating plans and activities and taking turns in conversation.	7, 10	CLL: Language for communication
Enjoy listening to and using spoken and written language, and readily turn to it in their play and learning.	2, 3, 4, 8, 9	
Sustain attentive listening, responding to what they have heard by relevant comments, questions or actions.	3, 4, 7, 8, 9, 10	
Listen with enjoyment, and respond to stories, songs and other music, rhymes and poems and make up their own stories, songs, rhymes and poems.	1, 3, 4, 6, 7, 8, 9, 10	
Extend their vocabulary, exploring the meanings and sounds of new words.	3, 7, 8, 10	
Speak clearly and audibly with confidence and control and show awareness of the listener, for example by their use of conventions such as greetings, 'please' and 'thank you'.	10	
Use language to imagine and recreate roles and experiences.	3, 8, 10	CLL: Language for thinking
Use talk to organize, sequence and clarify thinking, ideas, feelings and events.	10	

53

Early Learning Goals	Activity	Area of Learning
Explore and experiment with sounds, words and texts.	3, 8	CLL: Reading
Retell narratives in the correct sequence, drawing on language patterns of stories.	8, 9, 10	
Show an understanding of the elements of stories, such as main character, sequence of events, and openings, and how information can be found in non-fiction texts to answer questions about where, who, why and how.	8 ,10	
Find out about, and identify, some features of living things, objects and events they observe.	3, 9	KNU: Exploration and investigation
Look closely at similarities, differences, patterns and change.	3, 7	
Move with confidence, imagination and safety.	1, 2, 3, 6, 7, 8	PD: Movement
Move with control and co-ordination.	1, 2, 3, 6, 7, 8, 10	
Travel around, under, over and through balancing and climbing equipment.	8	
Show awareness of space, of themselves and of others.	1, 2, 3, 7, 8	PD: Sense of space
Recognize the change that happens to their bodies when they are active.	1, 7	PD: Health and bodily awareness
Use a range of small and large equipment.	5, 7	PD: Using equipment
Handle tools, objects, construction and malleable materials safely and with increasing control.	5, 9, 10	PD: Using tools and materials
Explore colour, texture, shape, form, space in two or three dimensions.	1, 2, 8, 9	CD: Exploring media and materials
Recognize and explore how sounds can be changed, sing simple songs from memory, recognize repeated sounds and sound patterns and match movements to music.	1, 2, 4, 5, 6, 7, 8	CD: Music
Use their imagination in art and design, music, dance, imaginative and role-play and stories.	1, 2, 3, 5, 6, 8, 10	CD: Imagination
Respond in a variety of ways to what they see, hear, smell, touch and feel.	4, 5, 6, 7	CD: Responding to experiences, and expressing and communicating ideas
Express and communicate their ideas, thoughts and feelings by using a widening range of materials, suitable tools, imaginative and role-play, movement, designing and making, and a variety of songs and musical instruments.	5, 7, 8, 9, 10	

CHAPTER 4

Visiting the Built Environment

> This chapter is divided into the following sections:
>
> ■ How the built environment can help young children learn
>
> ■ Trails: 12 trails focusing children on different elements of the built environment

Suggestions for activities that can be pursued in the setting are included throughout the chapter.

How the built environment can help children learn

The Commission for Architecture and the Built Environment (CABE) describes the built environment as 'the cities, towns and villages where we live and work: the buildings, the architecture and the spaces between them' (*Neighbourhood Journeys*, 2004, Foreword). This definition gives tremendous scope for children to explore their surroundings in an enjoyable way. By focusing on different elements of the built environment, children can begin to:

■ Appreciate their locality and the communities that live there. This in turn develops the children's own sense of place, and supports work in the area of citizenship.

■ Gain an understanding of heritage through buildings and monuments.

■ Understand principles of construction and design, and the use of different materials.

■ Learn that buildings and features of the built environment have functions which are often represented through their appearance.

■ Develop their literacy and numeracy skills through observing the words and numbers used in their locality.

Through exploring their built environment, children will also become more discerning about the design of buildings and their uses. You can develop this if you are making any aesthetic or structural changes to your own setting. Even very young children can contribute their ideas.

Trails

Trails offer a simple and effective starting point for developing children's appreciation of the built environment. On one level, trails can be viewed simply as going for a walk. On a more focused level, they direct children's learning in ways that can be developed later at the setting. Trails are most successful when they have a context which is clearly explained to the children before the walk and sustained while the walk is taking place.

Case Study 15

The built environment

Westminster Children's Society (WCS)

Westminster Children's Society believes in exploring the local community and its cultural heritage. The organization's chief executive describes an activity which grew from taking a short walk to the shops.

We go out of the setting at least once a week, sometimes more. We'll visit the local museum or art gallery, or we'll just go for a walk to observe what's going on in the street. We've talked with our children about different styles of architecture and they are now perfectly capable of noticing the difference between Georgian and Victorian architecture.

One day I took five children out with me to go to the shops, and on our way there we passed a building which had a lift on the outside of it, going up and down. The children were fascinated, and we stood and watched it for a while. Then we went into the building's foyer and I asked if we could have a go in the lift. The building's receptionist said that it wasn't possible to arrange this right away for health and safety reasons, but that we should come back the next day – so we did. We spent about 15 minutes just going up and down in the lift and talking about what we could see around us at the different levels. The views were amazing at the top of the building, but much more street life could be observed as the lift descended. When we got back to the setting the children each drew their favourite viewpoint.

---

1 Local area trail

Introducing the children in your setting to their immediate surroundings can be complemented with activities using maps and representations of local features. With all of the trails suggested in this chapter, it's useful to take with you clipboards, paper, pencils, a camera, and sound recording equipment if you have access to this. The children can capture elements of the surrounding area that interest them either by drawing, writing, taking photos or recording sounds. Adults can enhance the children's interest through unobtrusive discussion, and can act as scribes for children's comments when necessary.

It's important to plan the route in advance of the walk so that you are clear where you are going and what the health and safety issues may be. (Further practical information about taking children into the built environment is offered in Chapter 6.) During this reconnaissance trip, you can note features which can be drawn to the children's attention, and which might form the basis of effective follow-up activities. Jot down the route in the form of a map, so that the other adults can follow it when you all take the walk with the children.

While you are on the walk with the children, focus their attention on the elements of the built environment noted during the reconnaissance trip, and associate the features geographically to the setting:

- If you see tall houses nearby, you could ask the children if they think the setting could be seen from the top window of the house. Would it take long to walk to the setting from that house?

- Look at the local houses and other buildings, and introduce relevant vocabulary like 'chimney', 'roof', 'block' and 'estate'.

- Look at street names and street features, such as lamp posts and bus stops. Perhaps the street would look better with differently coloured bus stops. Which colours would the children prefer?

- What is the children's favourite part of the walk, and why?

- What additional features would the children like to see in the street?

Note the children's observations so that they can be represented on any work produced at the setting, such as a map.

4.1 Cruddas Park Early Years Centre's visit to Central Arcade

Making a map

Maps are useful in developing children's abstract awareness, and in serving as a reference and a reminder of the local area. A map can be as simple or elaborate as you and the children wish it to be. It might be developed over days or weeks, using two- and three-dimensional material. You can use a variety of media for the map, for example some white fabric for the background and fabric pens to make marks. Alternatively you can use large sheets of paper stuck together, enabling copies of the photographs taken during the walk to be placed at the relevant points on the map.

Prepare a simple map which shows the streets you all walked along and spread it on the floor. Start the process as a group activity, and talk with the children about what they remember from the walk. Make a note as they mention different features. The children can then put images and objects on to the map to represent the features they remember most vividly:

- Photos can be fixed in relevant places.

- Comments made by children during the walk can be written down and placed next to the relevant parts on the map.

- If the map can stay undisturbed in a safe area, three-dimensional materials such as building blocks or cardboard tubes and boxes can be used to represent buildings.

- Numbers and letters can indicate street numbers on houses or street names.

- Dangerous areas on the walk, such as busy roads, can be expressed by a symbol chosen by the children.

- Imaginary characters invented by the children can be represented on the map. You could discuss with the children why certain people live in certain places, and what their needs might be because of where they live.

- The children can make up stories about the area. Larger maps can be used for role-play, for example small play-people can be moved among the streets and buildings.

It's effective to take the children on the same trail for a second time during the period in which they are making the map. They will notice different features which can be added to the map on their return.

Map-making activities can also be applied to the trails outlined below. For example, children could choose how to represent on the map certain sounds they hear during the 'listening trail', or the colours they note during the 'colour trail'. A sturdy map showing the outline of the area is useful, because it can serve as a template for different map activities every time you take the children on a trail.

2 Materials trail

The built environment is rich with different materials, including:

- Natural stone (walls, kerb stones, some paving, façades of some civic buildings, for example marble)

- Bricks and other man-made materials (paving slabs, concrete, breeze blocks)

- Metal (roofs, bus shelters, street signs, lamp posts, pedestrian crossings)

- Wood (shop fronts, shop signs, doors, window frames, trees)

- Glass (windows, doors, walls, roofs)

- Plastic (advertising stands and billboards, stand-alone toilets)

- Fabric (shop awnings, banners)

Some buildings may be constructed from a combination of several different materials. Encourage the children to spot how many are used. Talk about the textures of the materials, and why each material has been chosen for its particular function. What would it be like if the road surface was made out of plastic, or if buildings were made out of fabric? Children can also consider the different elements of the built environment which are made of the same materials, such as roofs, walls and pavements.

This trail will be enhanced if you bring samples of different materials with you. The children can feel and look at the samples and then see if they can spot the material used in their immediate environment.

3 Heritage trail

This trail focuses on historical aspects of the built environment. These can include:

- Monuments and sculptures

- Plaques on buildings

- Fountains

- Original features on buildings, such as carved stonework and stained glass windows

- Cultural venues, for example museums, art galleries, and theatres

Observing these features can prompt discussion about the past and how our local environment changes. By looking at older buildings, children can begin to imagine what a street has looked like in earlier times.

You can prepare for the heritage trail by visiting your local authority's archives office or local history society to find old photographs of the streets you are going to explore. These can provide absorbing starting points for discussions about old and new buildings, and how people lived in the past. Discussions can focus on why some buildings survive while others are replaced. You could stand in front of two buildings, one old and one new, and talk about their differences. Some children may prefer the modern building, others the historic building. Find out what their preference is, and why.

Activities in the setting

Clay monuments and sculptures

Children are often fascinated by the scale and grandeur of historic monuments and sculptures, particularly if they can touch them. It is all the better if the children are able to climb, feel, hold, smell, and look at a monument or sculpture. This helps them to take the sensory experience back to their setting where they can extend and explore it further.

Silhouettes and shadows

On a sunny day, large monuments and sculptures can cast wonderful shadows, dwarfing small children. The shadows can be played with by children moving in, out of and around them. If you take some large sheets of paper with you on your trip, the children can lay them out beneath the monument or sculpture to capture its shadow, and draw around it to create a two-dimensional representation of what they are looking at. The results can then be taken back to the setting to be decorated with pastels and chalks or with collage pieces to raise the surface of the shadow, representing its original colour and texture.

Big clay models

Looking at big sculptures provides inspiration for the children to make their own large clay models in their setting, which serves to develop their visual and tactile awareness. Photographs and charcoal sketches produced during their visit will help to remind children of what they saw, and fire their imagination. Make sure the children have access to big lumps of clay (football-size) so that they can work with big shapes. Encourage them to handle the material in different ways and to appreciate that each finished sculpture is unique.

4 Places of worship trail

Seek out buildings devoted to worship. These could be:

- Churches and cathedrals of different denominations
- Synagogues
- Mosques
- Hindu temples
- Sikh gurdwaras
- Quaker meeting houses

There are many ways to focus children's learning through visiting places of worship. You can talk about the buildings' functions, how people behave inside them and why. The buildings are often ornate. Look at the features and talk about why extra care has been taken with them. Are there clues which indicate the building is used for worship? Try to find at least two different places of worship on your trail and compare them. Is one more ornate than the other? Quaker meeting houses are designed simply, whereas churches are often resplendent with stained glass windows and decorated internal features. You can also look at how the buildings differ in shape. Temple roofs can consist of impressive domes, and some churches have spires. Windows, doors and internal features can also prompt discussion about shape and function.

Case Study 16

Visit to a Catholic cathedral

Our Lady and St Anne's Roman Catholic Primary School

Northern Architecture and Sightlines Initiative co-ordinated a project called City Sense, involving four Early Years settings and students from the Architecture Department of Newcastle University. The scheme was funded by Newcastle New Deal for Communities (Community Chest Grant). Adults and children together visited sites in the city, each chosen for their architectural interest and their sense of place. This visit involved twenty two children aged 4 and 5 years old, accompanied by eleven adult helpers.

The cathedral is situated near to the setting, and the group took a minibus to get there. As soon as the children approached the cathedral they were full of ideas and questions. They were interested in many elements of the cathedral, including the use of the building, the decorations, the sculptures, the floor, doors and windows. A great deal of discussion took place during the visit and lots of digital photographs were taken.

Follow-up work at the setting revealed the positive impact the visit made on the children. This included:

Stories: Adults transcribed stories told by the children about the cathedral, and these were made into a storybook. One story described a giant who lived in the cathedral. Another was based on a bird, inspired by a large gargoyle on the building's exterior. One child, convinced that he could see the design of crocodiles included in the ornate metal grating on part of the cathedral floor, created a story about the crocodile in the cathedral.

Drama and dance: The children acted out their stories and created narrative dance pieces to accompany the drama.

Model cathedrals and features: Many of the children made their own cathedrals and decorated them. The children's creative ideas were inspired by their visit. The model-making activity also prompted personal, social and emotional development, as children invited others to help decorate the model cathedrals they had made. Children made other models using wooden bricks.

Tile patterns: Referring to digital images of the floor of the cathedral, the children recreated the patterns using the plastic tile pattern boards at the setting. A table for cutting and sticking was also prepared, and the many photos from the visit were put on it. The children responded to these and created their own patterned collages.

Slide show: All the digital photographs taken during the visit were collated into a slide show. The children watched this frequently.

Display: The work produced by the children described above culminated in a rich visual display which was available for the other children in the setting to look at.

Practitioners at the setting have been delighted with the imaginative content of the stories and artwork produced by the children. They are keen to make visits to other buildings to sustain the children's obvious interest in this subject.

Activities in the setting

Stained glass windows

If the children have been lucky enough to view some stained glass windows on their trip, they can use tissue paper and cellophane to make their own colourful windows. If there are big, low windows at the setting, allow the children plenty of space to spread the coloured paper out and attach it to the inside of the windows using Blu-Tack, Sellotape or washable glue. Black lines can be painted for the stained glass window effect, or you can use thin strips of black card. The effects can be enjoyed from either side of the window.

5 Colour trail

Play a game with the children where each person in turn chooses a colour which everyone must then find somewhere in the street. Encourage children to look for colours appearing in street features rather than in clothes worn by passers-by. Street signs, shop fronts and displays, street furniture, brickwork and building features show colours that can be spotted by even the youngest children. Discuss shades of colour, and explore more detailed ways of describing the colours the children have observed, for example by matching the colour to an object or feature, such as 'pea-green', 'sky-blue' or 'brick-red'.

6 Listening trail

Focus the children's attention on what they can hear as they walk within their local built environment. If they are sidetracked into noticing visual elements of the environment, encourage them to consider how what they have observed might sound. Natural sounds, such as birds singing or the wind moving through trees, can be heard in context with other, more urban sounds. How easy is it to hear the birds singing over the sound of the traffic? Ask the children to count how many sounds they can hear simultaneously. Examples might include:

- Buildings' features. These can include clocks chiming, doors opening and closing and doorbells ringing.

- Traffic. Children can classify different types of vehicles, for example cars, emergency services, buses and bicycles. If they listen very carefully, with their eyes closed, they might be able to work out the movement of the traffic: cars stopping then starting again, or a bus at a bus stop letting people on and off.

- People. Children might hear people talking, or tradespeople such as newspaper vendors calling out to passers-by.

- Natural sounds. Careful listening can locate sounds of nature, such as the wind, birds singing or, if you are near water, the flow of a river or the sea.

- Other sounds can include the short regular tones heard at a pedestrian crossing, cars hooting and shop doors opening and closing.

This activity develops listening skills and heightens appreciation of the built environment generally. You can use the listening trail to discuss with the children what it must be like to rely on sounds alone, as is the case for blind people. You can also encourage children to use their sense of smell. The aromas they smell during their walk can be incorporated into the map-making activity described earlier in this chapter. The trail also offers an ideal opportunity for the children to capture the sounds using recording equipment. The recordings made can be used in different ways in the setting, for example as an aide-mémoire or as the basis for creative work such as music composition.

Activities in the setting

Having focused on sounds during different trails, the children can then explore the external sound environment of their setting. This is possible whatever the size or shape of the outside space.

Go for a blindfold walk

Children can do this in pairs, taking it in turns to be leader and follower. Having fixed a blindfold on to the follower, the leader then proceeds to take their partner around the outside space, encouraging them to stop at and feel interesting things on their way. The follower can try to recognize other children's voices and the different play areas as they approach them.

Sound bingo

Spend time in the outside area of your setting making cards to symbolize different sounds that have been identified by the children (what children pick out may be different from what adults pick out). Examples may be birdsong, car horns, children playing on bicycles, children playing with sand or water, etc. Encourage the children to design symbols which represent these sounds. Once you are sure that all the children are familiar with what the symbols represent, they can be photocopied to make bingo cards. Play bingo outside with the children listening to the sounds around them and seeing who can fill in their card first.

Guess the sound

If you can, obtain sound recording equipment and a digital camera for the children to take outside to record and take photographs of what is happening around them. Using this recorded evidence, set up a 'guess the sound' game, where children have to match the sound recorded with the correct picture taken with the camera. This game develops visual and listening skills effectively.

7 Transport trail: bridges and stations

Utilitarian features of the built environment, such as bridges and train stations, are structures we can tend to take for granted. However, these features are often examples of magnificent architecture and engineering. Some train stations, both historic and contemporary, can be viewed as industrial cathedrals, displaying enormous arches and ornate designs. It is well worth arranging a visit to such a train station to look at the architecture alone, but you can also use the visit as a basis for further work on trains and transport in general.

4.2 Follow-up bridges art activity at Walkergate Early Years Centre

Looking at bridges can stimulate a range of activities in the setting. Case Study 17 describes the follow-up work a group of children undertook with great interest and enthusiasm after a visit to some bridges. If your setting is not close to a bridge of interest, you can arrange a trip to see one in the region, treating the visit as though it were to a cultural venue. If any parent is a builder, structural engineer or architect, you could ask them if they would accompany you on the visit to talk about the materials, the construction or the design of the bridge. You can read stories featuring bridges to the children to spark their imagination and curiosity before the visit.

Case Study 17

Bridges

Walkergate Early Years Centre, Newcastle-upon-Tyne

In this case study the practitioner demonstrates how responding to the interests of the children can provide opportunities for high levels of engagement and creative thinking. The children were also able to become more familiar with their local environment, experiment freely with materials and develop their ability to work in groups.

We observed the children's interest in the Tyne bridges during a coach journey to the theatre, so we decided to take a closer look at the bridges across the River Tyne in Newcastle and Gateshead. The children were also involved in a school project looking at the local environment and community, and they enjoy construction activities generally. We thought that a visit to the bridges would be a good stimulus for their building skills.

Case Study *continued*

We hired a minibus and took eight children and four adults to see the bridges. The visit included walking across the Millennium Bridge and looking at model bridges in the Gateshead Visitor Centre. The children were provided with clipboards and made sketches of the bridges. We documented the visit by taking digital photographs and recording the children's dialogue throughout the journey and while observing the river and various bridges. We discovered the imaginative journeys children take when they look at bridges and buildings; they saw human or animal characteristics within the structures, like a giant, a whale and an octopus.

The children were highly motivated by the visit and a great deal of related work was generated afterwards at the setting. The digital images and other documentation were displayed to help the children remember the trip. The children created wonderful representations of the images through drawings, paintings, collage work, model-making and construction work. The images were a source of interest to the other children, so we organized two more visits with different groups of children.

To extend the children's thinking we planned some problem-solving activities, where they were asked to make something to help a play-person get across the river. Ideas and models generated by the children included stepping stones, bridges, ships, aeroplanes, ladders and drawbridges. A teacher also made up a story about the medieval bridge to help the children understand some historical facts about their local area. A nursery nurse illustrated the main characters, and the children made their own drawings in response.

We also encouraged the children to explore, choose and test out different materials for their models. The range of materials they chose to use included willow, masking tape, wire, paper clips, pipe-cleaners, string, art straws, glue, wood, Pritt Stick, corks, lolly sticks, a range of boxes and other recycled materials. The children used their skills of fastening, cutting and estimating during this activity.

The first group co-operated with each other to make a model of the river and its bridges, and included their own ideas and designs. Some children made individual models. Another group built a huge bridge with boxes and other materials. For a while in the setting, there appeared to be bridges everywhere!

We have been very excited by the impact of the experience on the children's learning. The children have learnt a lot about their local environment. They have also remembered the names of all the bridges and some of the key buildings such as the BALTIC centre for contemporary art and the Sage Gateshead music venue.

8 Shops trail

Looking at shops and shop fronts offers children the chance to explore design and functionality. Children can identify what each shop is selling. Together you can talk about the displays in shop windows and why the goods might have been laid out in the way they have. Look at the design of the shops' entrances. Are they inviting? How easy is it to walk in and take a closer look at what's on offer? What can you tell about the neighbourhood by looking at the shops? Is it a shopping area, or are there just a few shops on the street selling essential items?

If it can be arranged, ask shop staff beforehand if they would mind spending a few minutes talking with the children about the way the shop is designed and how it seeks to attract customers.

Case Study 18

Newcastle Central Arcade

Cruddas Park Early Years Centre, Newcastle

This visit was made under the Northern Architecture and Sightlines Initiative co-ordinated the collaborative project City Sense, described in the Case Study 16. A group of six children aged 3 and 4 visited Newcastle's Edwardian shopping centre, Central Arcade. The visit was followed up by three sessions in the setting.

Central Arcade was chosen as a venue of interest because of its ornate decoration and glass barrel-vaulted roof. The floor is tiled throughout, and sculptural details can be seen high up. However, the children's focus was entirely upon features at eye and ground level. The mosaic floor, with its Greek key border and central circle, floor's interested the group most. The children congregated in the circle and represented the strong graphic shapes in their drawings. At the adults' suggestion, the children made rubbings of the floor's patterns using paper and charcoal. Other areas of fascination for the children were the displays in the shop windows and the shops' smells. The accompanying adults noticed that the children's exploration of the space was sensory and physical; they looked, touched, smelled, knelt and lay in the space.

Follow-up work in the setting developed the children's interest by recreating the circle that had featured on the arcade's floor. Large sheets of brown paper were joined together to form one piece, on which a circle was drawn. The children sat within the circle and created patterns and shapes with the different tiled mosaics, glass beads and coloured stones placed there. The children had taken photographs during their visit and recaptured their memories by looking at the prints.

The visiting group did not experience any practical difficulties, despite the public character of the venue. The Foundation Stage co-ordinator felt that the visit to Central Arcade supported the children's learning, introduced them to a new and stimulating environment, and provided a rich experience that could be developed further in the setting.

4.3 Cruddas, Park Early Years Centre's visit to Central Arcade

Activities in the setting

Model streets and mini-environments

After looking at the different shop fronts and their various features, characters and sounds, recreate the environment within the setting. Set up a model street with the children, in which they can move around. Use a variety of junk boxes and containers to represent shops and buildings. This model street can lead to effective role-play such as money handling and exploration of character. It also reinforces the development of literacy through the use of signs, receipts and advertisements.

This activity can also be recreated on a smaller scale with little boxes and small-world equipment so that the children make a mini-environment. This works indoors and outdoors, and can lead to creative small group storytelling and role-play.

9 Building works trail

Locate a building site where you can watch the work and discuss it with the children. Is a new building being constructed? If so, what was there before? If a building is being renovated, which parts are changing? Why has it been decided to renovate rather than construct a new building in the same place? Is the building being cleaned? What makes buildings dirty? What building materials can the children see? How do the builders know what to do?

This trail can be enhanced either before or after the walk if you can invite a builder or an architect into your setting to talk with the children about what they do and why. Alternatively, you might find a friendly site manager who can speak to the children at the building site.

Activities in the setting

Building works

A visit to a building site provides a strong stimulus for imaginative role-play within the setting. Plan the building works role-play area with the children so that they contribute in the light of what they have observed during their visit. You can transform a space inside or outside your setting into a building site which could include:

- Hard hats (these can be bought from educational suppliers)

- Scaffolding (this is included in construction kit equipment available from educational suppliers)

- Bricks (for example, toy construction bricks)

- Buckets and spades

- A cement mixer (this can be a simple container holding either imaginary cement or a mix of flour and water, depending on how messy you want the activity to become!)

- Wellies

- Measuring equipment

10 Words, numbers and symbols trail

Street environments are rich with words, numbers and symbols. Encourage the children to seek them out and, if practical, copy them using clipboards, paper and pencils. Children need to look high up and low down, as well as at their own eye-level. Ask the children about why the words, numbers or symbols are there. There could be a variety of reasons:

Words

- To indicate the names of the streets. What would happen if street names were removed? Does the name of the street tell us anything about the area?

- To communicate to people what the building is for. Are there other ways people can tell what a shop is selling other than by the words? Is there a company's name on the building? How is it displayed?

- To indicate ownership, for example local council emblems on rubbish bins. Is the council the only agency responsible for rubbish in the environment? How can we contribute to keeping the area clean and tidy?

- To commemorate events or people. Who once lived in the building or street? Do we know what happened here in the past?

- To give directions, for example for cars parking, drivers or pedestrians on the move. How else might people find their way to where they want to go?

Numbers

- To inform people about bus routes and times. How would people know where and when to go if there were no numbers? How many buses use this bus stop? How frequently do they stop here?

- To show what time it is. Is the clock high up or low down? Why is it useful high up?

- To help people find the right building. Where are building numbers indicated on the building? Is it easy or difficult to see the number? What is the highest number on the street?

- To show when something was built. Is there a date on the building? Why is it useful or interesting to know when something was built? How is the date displayed?

Symbols

- To communicate a direction. Look at the walking green man at a pedestrian crossing. Is this symbol better than using a word like 'walk'? Would someone who doesn't speak English understand the direction? Talk about pictures and how these can be just as useful as words, if not more so.

- To indicate a mode of transport. Is the same symbol on all the bus/metro/tram stops? Are there parts of the road which are reserved for bicycles? How can you tell?

- To show where vehicles can and cannot park. Where are the clues? Look on the ground and on nearby signs. Do we have to know what the symbols mean to understand the instructions?

11 Inside buildings trail

Drawing children's attention to the architectural and decorative detail within a building will help them understand the building's past and engage with aesthetic elements that can help develop awareness of shape, pattern and colour. These elements are immediately accessible in historic country houses, but they can also be seen in period shopping arcades and town halls. Provided you have been granted permission and have thought through health and safety considerations, it can be more instructive and enjoyable to lie down on the floor of the building and look upwards, than to stand up craning your necks.

Case Study 19

Visit to Leighton House

Chelsea Open Air Nursery School

The practitioner at Chelsea Open Air Nursery School describes how the children reacted when they visited the Arab Hall at Leighton House.

I set the scene to move to the Arab Hall so we all metaphorically climbed on to a magic carpet and went travelling to a country with a desert where creatures such as 'camels, snakes and insects lived' and where the 'sun shone all day'.

As we walked in, the calm atmosphere instantly subdued the children. They settled on the rugs surrounding the pool and at my suggestion laid back to look up at the ceiling. The room is like a temple or shrine. It is decorated in tiles of blue, green, turquoise, gold and white. Around the walls are creatures such as peacocks, camels, fish, mermaids (who were 'like Barbie!'), ancient galleons and Arabic script. Above the pool is a glittering candelabrum which lights up the multi-domed ceiling and the surrounding stained glass windows creating strange effects with colour and light. The children commented: 'I can see a flower'. 'And a peacock'. Another said, 'I can see all different colours with that light'.

The dialogue was diverse and interesting, as it was about the tiles themselves, which the children were later asked to record by drawing using felt-tip pens. While the children drew, their verbal observations flowed (some self-initiated and some encouraged by adult questioning). These included the fact that one child knew that the writing was Arabic from his attendance at a religious Saturday School: 'There is writing there like when I go to my Saturday School!'

Activities in the setting

Jigsaw pictures

This activity is for children who lay down during a visit to a building. Let them adopt the same position as they did at the visited building, lying flat on the ground, gazing up. This can be done in any space in the setting, including the role-play areas which may have suspended patterned fabric and other decorative features fixed to the ceiling. Pass round a digital camera so that children can each take one or two photographs of what they see above them. Once the photographs have been printed, encourage the children to put them together like a jigsaw so that the ceiling is recreated on the floor. By spending time looking around them in this way, the children can consider how the features of indoor environments can be changed. They may suggest their own ideas, which can be incorporated within the setting.

12 Rural built environment trail

You don't need to have access to busy urban environments to appreciate architecture. The countryside offers opportunities to observe buildings and other features that often exist to serve the rural community, like farms and village greens. Many historic buildings such as castles and forts still stand in the countryside, prompting discussions about the past. Clues to the country's industrial heritage can still be found in many areas, for example disused railway lines and mines.

While in the countryside, you can also discuss with children architectural features they may recognize from their local environment, such as thatch on cottages or the use of black beams in Tudor-era buildings. Road signs and road markings will differ subtly from those in busier urban environments. If it's possible, arrange visits to rural and urban environments to give the children scope to compare the two.

Case Study 20

Greenhead to Thirlwall Toddler Walks

Children from Greenhead First School participate annually in a walk organized by the Hadrian's Wall Tourism Partnership (HWTP). The walk is funded by the HWTP and the Heritage Lottery Fund. Below is HWTP's own description of the event, which demonstrates how young children can respond to the built environment within a rural setting. The activity accommodates up to seventeen children with ten adult helpers.

The route follows the road to Glenwhelt Farm, goes through the farmyard and north to the steep pastures around Holmhead, across three steep ladder stiles to Duffenfoot and then up to Thirlwall Castle where storytelling activities take place. The route back follows the footpath beside the railway line, through Greenhead village, past the Youth Hostel and back to the school. The walk starts at 9.30 and finishes at 11.30.

The excitement and adventure of this big group walk for these young children is always palpable. They chat to each other about everything they can see and are attentive and watchful at each stopping place. These young children enjoy the activity of walking through the pastures to the castle and being out with their peer group and accompanying adults. They like watching the landscape change, talking about the colours they can see, the shadow of the clouds moving across the fields, and the ruin of Thirlwall looming in the near distance. In turn, there are a few stops where the leader talks about the castle's history and more recent past, and of the railway, local quarrying and mining and the area's industrial history.

So far, everyone has managed this one-mile off-road circular walk with a little help getting over stiles, and there have been no major health and safety incidents. The route is quite exciting with a farmyard to cross, a boggy path section to navigate, narrow paths through hill pastures, a stream to cross by footbridge and then a steep climb to the castle itself. The return route is along a narrow path beside a railway line carrying the Newcastle–Carlisle trains, which can be noisy and exciting!

Curriculum Links

1. Making a map

2. Materials trail

3. Heritage trail

4. Silhouettes and shadows

5. Big clay models

6. Places of worship trail

7. Stained glass windows

8. Colour trail

9. Listening trail

10. Blindfold walk

11. Sound bingo

12. Guess the sound

13. Shops trail

14. Model streets and mini-environments

15. Building works

16. Words, numbers and symbols trail

17. Inside buildings trail

18. Jigsaw pictures

Early Learning Goals	Activity	Area of Learning
Continue to be interested, excited and motivated to learn.	All	PSE: Dispositions and attitudes
Be confident to try out new activities, indicate ideas and speak in a familiar group.	All	
Respond to significant experiences, showing a range of feelings when appropriate.	1, 4, 9	PSE: Self-confidence and self-esteem
Have a developing awareness of their own needs, views and feelings and be sensitive to the needs, views and feelings of others.	1, 6, 9, 14, 16	
Have a developing respect for their own cultures and beliefs and those of others.	1, 6	
Form good relationships with adults and peers.	2, 3, 8	PSE: Making relationships
Work as part of a group or class, taking turns and sharing fairly, understanding that there needs to be agreed values and codes of behaviour for groups of people, including adults and children, to work together harmoniously.	9, 10, 14	
Consider the consequences of their words and actions for themselves and others.	9	PSE: Behaviour and self-control
Understand that people have different needs, views, cultures and beliefs, that need to be treated with respect.	6, 10, 15	PSE: Sense of community
Understand that they can expect others to treat their needs, views, cultures and beliefs with respect.	6, 10, 15	
Interact with others, negotiating plans and activities and taking turns in conversation.	10	CLL: Language for communication
Sustain attentive listening, responding to what they have heard by relevant comments, questions or actions.	9, 10	
Extend their vocabulary, exploring the meanings and sounds of new words.	1, 11, 16	
Use language to imagine and recreate roles and experiences.	1, 15	CLL: Language for thinking
Use talk to organize, sequence and clarify thinking, ideas, feelings and events.	1	
Link sounds to letters, naming and sounding the letters of the alphabet.	16	CLL: Linking sounds and letters
Use their phonic knowledge to write simple regular words and make phonetically plausible attempts at more complex words.	1, 16	
Explore and experiment with sounds, words and texts.	1, 11, 16	CLL: Reading
Show an understanding of the elements of stories, such as main character, sequence of events, and openings, and how information can be found in non-fiction texts to answer questions about where, who, why and how.	14, 15	

Early Learning Goals	Activity	Area of Learning
Attempt writing for different purposes, using features of different forms such as lists, stories and instructions.	1, 11, 14, 16	CLL: Writing
Write their own names and other things such as labels and captions and begin to form simple sentences, sometimes using punctuation.	1, 14, 16	
Say and use number names in order in familiar contexts.	1, 14, 16	MD: Numbers as labels and for counting
Count reliably up to 10 everyday objects.	1	
Recognize numerals 1 to 9.	1, 16	
Use language such as 'greater', 'smaller', 'heavier' or 'lighter' to compare quantities.	5	MD: Shape, space and measure
Talk about and recognize and recreate simple patterns.	1, 17, 18	
Use language such as 'circle', 'bigger' to describe the shape and size of solids and flat shapes.	5, 17	
Use everyday words to describe position.	1, 11, 12, 17, 18	
Investigate objects and materials by using all their senses as appropriate.	1, 2, 4, 5, 8, 9, 10, 11, 12	KNU: Exploration and investigation
Find out more about and identify some features of living things, objects and events they observe.	1, 2, 4, 5, 8, 9, 11, 12, 14	
Look closely at similarities, differences, patterns and change.	6, 7, 17, 18	
Ask questions about why things happen and how things work.	1, 2, 12, 14, 16, 17, 18	
Build and construct with a wide range of objects, selecting appropriate resources, and adapting their work where necessary.	1, 5, 14, 15	KNU: Designing and making skills.
Select the tools and techniques they need to shape, assemble and join materials they are using.	1, 5, 14	
Find out about and identify the uses of everyday technology and use information and communication technology and programmable toys to support their learning.	12, 15	KNU: Information and communication technology
Find out about past and present events in their own lives, and those of their families and other people they know.	1, 2, 3, 14	KNU: Sense of time
Observe, find out about and identify features in the place they live and the natural world.	All	KNU: Sense of place
Find out about their environment, and talk about those features they like and dislike.	1, 2, 7, 4, 9, 14, 17, 18	
Begin to know about their own cultures and beliefs and those of other people.	6, 13, 14	KNU: Cultures and beliefs

▶

Early Learning Goals	Activity	Area of Learning
Move with confidence, imagination and safety. Move with control and co-ordination.	1, 9, 10, 14, 15, 1, 10, 14	PD: Movement
Show awareness of space, of themselves and of others.	4, 10, 14, 17, 18	PD: Sense of space
Recognize the change that happens to their bodies when they are active.	4	PD: Health and bodily awareness
Use a range of small and large equipment.	12, 14, 15	PD: Using equipment
Handle tools, objects, construction and malleable materials safely and with increasing control.	5, 12, 14, 15	PD: Using tools and materials
Explore colour, texture, shape, form, space in two or three dimensions.	1, 3, 4, 5, 8, 11, 12, 14, 17, 18	CD: Exploring media and materials
Use their imagination in art and design, music, dance, imaginative and role-play and stories.	1, 14, 15	CD: Imagination
Respond in a variety of ways to what they see, hear, smell, touch and feel. Express and communicate their ideas, thoughts and feelings by using a widening range of materials, suitable tools, imaginative and role-play, movement, designing and making, and a variety of songs and musical instruments.	2, 4, 5, 8, 9, 10, 11, 12, 17, 18 4, 5, 14	CD: Responding to experiences, and expressing and communicating ideas

CHAPTER 5

Visiting Zoos, Farms and Aquariums

> This chapter is divided into the following sections:
>
> ■ How zoos, farms and aquariums can help young children learn
>
> ■ Zoos: Before the visit and On the day
>
> ■ Farms: Before the visit and On the day
>
> ■ Aquariums: Before the visit
>
> ■ After the visit

How zoos, farms and aquariums can help young children learn

Zoos, farms and aquariums offer children a rare chance to study living animals closely. Aside from creating excitement in children, these experiences can stimulate children's interest in the animal kingdom, and enable them to appreciate at first hand concepts central to the topics of Animals, Growth and Growing, Spring and Water. Comparisons between themselves and the animals enable children to understand more about human life, and how humans constitute just a fraction of life on this planet. Important conservation issues can be highlighted, through the work that zoos and farms are increasingly beginning to undertake in this area. Birth, babies and nurture can be a source of fascination, and may prompt you to discuss these matters with the children.

Zoos

The notion of a traditional zoo conjures up images of wild animals trapped in small enclosures. Fortunately this is no longer the case with many zoos in the United Kingdom. At their best, zoos are now more like small safari parks, with expanded living quarters for the animals and informed breeding programmes. Zoos devote much of their resources to promoting the importance of wildlife conservation, and many zoos support research departments. Education is a priority for all zoos, and many offer especially tailored sessions for Early Years. In the absence of such sessions, it is still valuable for young children to spend time looking at animals eating, sleeping or moving around their enclosures.

Before the visit

It's a good idea to make time to visit the zoo before the day of the trip so that you can learn which animals are kept there. This will help you to plan activities for the children before their own visit. During your familiarization visit, find out if the zoo caters for Early Years, as many will offer special sessions which you can integrate into the children's overall experience. It will also help your preparation if you pick up a map which shows the layout of the animal enclosures.

If you plan to prepare trails like the ones suggested in this chapter, find out if the zoo shop sells postcards or books which show the different animals. These can be used as images for the trails, and also as prompts for discussion with the children before the day of their visit.

Storybooks and discussion

Pick out any books at your setting that feature the animals which the children will be seeing at the zoo. Reading these with the children before the visit can provide useful information about the habits and habitats of the animals. Talk with children about how the animals move and what their skin or fur is like, including how they are coloured or patterned. You can follow these discussions with any of the pre-visit activities suggested below.

How do we move?

This is an energetic activity which requires a wide open space so that the children can move around freely. Talk with the children about different ways animals move. These might include:

- Flying (birds)
- Crawling (insects)
- Swimming (fish)
- Jumping (kangaroos)
- Leaping (monkeys)
- Slithering (snakes)
- Running (leopards)
- Walking (tortoises)

Children can suggest different animals for each type of movement, or you can suggest the animals listed above if a prompt is needed. Talk about why the animal moves like it does, such as:

- What does a bird need to be able to fly? (Wings)
- Why does a snake slither rather than walk? (Because it doesn't have legs or feet)
- Why is it useful for a monkey to leap from tree to tree? (To escape predators)

After this discussion, the children can try moving like the animals.

Animal skins feely bags

Prepare some feely bags, each of which contains a different type of animal skin. The skins don't have to be real. They can represent the different types of animal skin the children will see on animals at the zoo, for example:

- Fur: fake fur from a fabric sample

- Scales: cut up small strips of paper and stick the end of each of these together closely on to a piece of card

- Wool: cut up small lengths of wool and stick them closely on to a piece of card

- Shell: a seashell or fake tortoiseshell

- Feathers: these can be bought from educational suppliers

Encourage the children to take it in turns to feel in the bag and guess which animal skin is inside. They can then take it out of the bag and together you can talk about the nature of the skin.

- Is the skin soft or hard?

- Is the skin scaly or smooth?

- Which animal might have skin like this?

- How does the skin compare to our own skin?

Animal sounds

Discuss with the children the different sounds they might hear at the zoo. A good starting point is to talk about the sounds humans make. We talk, laugh, cry, shout and scream. Try these out with the children. Animals make a range of sounds too. Talk about these different sounds with the children, encouraging everyone to practise making the noises as loudly or as quietly as they can. Sounds might include:

- Tweeting (birds)

- Chattering (monkeys)

- Trumpeting (elephants)

- Growling (bears)

- Roaring (lions and tigers)

- Hissing (snakes)

You can raise or lower the volume of the noises by devising two signals, one representing 'quieter' and one representing 'louder', as in Case Study 10 on page 41.

Activity extension: animal stories

Make up a simple story with the children about an animal encountering other animals at the zoo. Each time a new animal is introduced into the story, the children can make the relevant sounds.

On the day

You can prepare in advance of the visit some simple activities which can focus the children's attention in different ways. These activities can take the form of trails, similar to those described in Case Study 21.

Colour trail

You will need:

- A transparent plastic bag.

- Different coloured small strips of card to put in the bag. Try to include at least five different colours, with ten pieces of each. This means you will have about 50 small strips of coloured card.

- Ten envelopes.

- A pen.

When you are looking at a particular enclosure during your visit, play a game with the children where they pick out colours from the bag which match the colours of the animals they are observing. Sometimes this will amount to just two or three colours, but if they are looking at brightly coloured birds, for example, there may be more. After the children have spotted all the colours, they can put the representative strips of card into one of the envelopes, which can be labelled using writing or pictures to indicate to which animal the colours correspond. You should keep these envelopes, as they can be useful for follow-up activities at the setting.

Pattern trail

This activity is similar to the colour trail described above, but it requires a little more preparation on your part. Before the children's visit, design some patterns which correspond to the skins of the animals the children will see at the zoo. Try to provide two of each pattern. These might include:

- Defined spots (leopard)

- Patches: large (giraffe)

- Patches: small (tortoise)

- Defined stripes: thick (tiger)

- Defined stripes: thin (zebra)

- No pattern (panther)

Design your pattern cards in black and white. As with the colour trail, you can ask the children to select the pattern card which corresponds most closely to the animal in that particular enclosure. It doesn't matter if the children can't decide between, for example, the thin stripes or the thick stripes when looking at the cards and the animal in question. It will prompt discussion and closer observation of the animals as a result. The children can colour in the pattern once they have matched it to the animal. Put the pattern card into an envelope and indicate which animal the card represents so that you can refer to it in the setting.

Case Study 21

Visit to Paignton Zoo

Highweek Community Nursery and Primary School

Highweek Community Nursery classes make frequent visits to different venues. They are fortunate in having the opportunity to borrow minibuses from two local secondary schools. This reduces the cost for the children's parents, most of whom live in an area of social deprivation.

The children make the trip to Paignton Zoo once every term. Twenty-six 4-year-olds visit in the morning, and the same number of 3-year-olds in the afternoon. As many as twenty adults accompany each group; parents are keen to visit themselves as well as to share responsibility for the children's welfare.

At the time of booking the visit, the practitioners know which topic they will be covering with the children at the setting. Paignton Zoo responds by providing relevant activities which the four-year-olds will enjoy when they reach the zoo. For their most recent visit, the children were investigating colour and pattern. The staff at Paignton Zoo have developed activities around camouflage and pattern, and have extended these so that they are integrated into the children's visit. The children were challenged to find animals with colours and patterns that matched the cards given to them. When the children located a correlating colour or pattern, they could post their cards into special post boxes which had been fixed by the enclosures. This encouraged the children to observe closely many of the animals' markings. The zoo provided a similar activity which involved the children investigating the topic New Life. Children were given pictures of baby animals, which they could then spot in the enclosures.

The 3-year-olds don't attend the session offered by the zoo because the practitioners have found that they respond better to a self-guided visit. Together, the group plans the route, using the map of the zoo to choose which animals to visit.

On return to the setting, the children make a book which records their visit, containing photos taken during the trip and the children's illustrations and comments. Each child can take the book home to show their parents. The children also build their own mini-zoos, and play out their visit and their own stories, using toy animals and models. Art activities include printing animal shapes hidden in splashes of colour, to show the effectiveness of camouflage. The children also enjoy looking at non-fiction books which reinforce their interest in the animals they saw at the zoo, and provide illustrations of the animals' natural habitats. This is of great interest to the children, many of whom were unaware that animals lived anywhere other than in a zoo!

Sounds trail

All you need for this activity is a map of the zoo and your ears. When the children are at a particular animal enclosure, encourage them to close their eyes and listen to the sounds that they hear. Find out whether they can copy the sound (quietly!), or describe in words (for example, 'screechy', 'roar', 'tweet tweet'). Make a note on the map which sounds were heard and where.

Case Study 22

Visit to Belfast Zoo

Ligoniel Primary School, Belfast

Seventeen children aged 4 and 5 visited Belfast Zoo, accompanied by five adults. The visit was part of their spring topics Animals and New Life, which had been organized at the beginning of the autumn term to ensure that the children could make the trip during the zoo's summer season. At this early stage, the practitioner received ideas for activities from the zoo, which included descriptions of the animals the children would see and suggestions for teaching links.

On the day of the visit, the children attended a special workshop led by an education officer at the zoo. They handled various animals such as rabbits, snakes and spiders. They were encouraged to ask questions that prompted animated discussions about habitats and how they might nurture the animals that they had handled.

The children had plenty of time to look at the animals in the zoo's enclosures. Their focus was influenced by their work at their setting, which in this case was about colour. They looked at the giraffe's skin and talked about the different shades of yellow and brown. However, the visit also depended on the children's own interests, which took discussion in other directions. The accompanying adults responded appropriately, allowing the visit to be led by the children's curiosity as much as by adult guidance.

On return to their setting, the children recorded their visit by creating large collaborative artwork. This was preceded by discussion about the animals seen at the zoo, which gave the children a context for their creative work. Pictures of various environments formed the background of the frieze paper used for the artwork, and children discussed with the practitioners why certain animals should be placed in particular habitats, such as bears occupying the wooded area.

The visit to Belfast Zoo and the accompanying activities stimulated the children's imaginations and stayed in their memories. The practitioner noticed that after the visit, children's motivation was raised when they looked at non-fiction books about animals.

Farms

In an educational context, farms offer a complement or an alternative to zoos, introducing children to farming life and domestic live animals. Children's first encounters with the animals on the farm may remain in their memories for ever, and can contribute to the children's understanding of the origins of common food products such as milk, butter, cheese and eggs. The animals on farms are often friendly, and will allow children to pet them. They can even be fed, if the rules allow it. Typically, farms will include some or all of the following:

5.1 Woodmansterne Primary School's visit to Bocketts Farm

- Chickens and other fowl
- Rabbits
- Guinea pigs
- Goats
- Sheep
- Pigs
- Donkeys
- Cows

Some farms keep rare breeds, and many run breeding programmes that enable groups to meet baby animals on their visit.

Before the visit

Familiarizing children with farm animals

If the children are unfamiliar with farm animals, find such animals in storybooks at your setting and talk to the children about the animals' different characteristics. Show illustrations of them and their babies when you can. Your discussion can include:

- The name of the animal (chicken)

- What its skin is like (covered with feathers)

- Why it lives on the farm (because it produces eggs)

- The noise that it makes (cluck cluck)

- What kind of habitat it has on the farm (coop)

- What its babies are called (chicks)

- What the babies look like (small and fluffy)

You can encourage children to imitate the sounds and movements of the animal as you discuss its characteristics.

Singing songs like 'Old MacDonald had a farm' and 'Baa baa black sheep' will also help familiarize the children with farm animals.

Who am I?

This game involves one child naming the characteristics of an animal and asking the others in the group to guess which animal is being described.

You will need:

- A drawstring bag

- Picture cards of animals, with one animal on each card (these can be bought from educational suppliers or you can draw the animals yourself)

You can begin the activity by showing the children how the game works. Pull out a picture card and make statements about the characteristics of the animal on the card until the children guess which animal you are describing. For example:

- I have four legs and a tail.

- I like eating grass.

- I produce milk.

- I can be black and white. I can also be brown.

- My babies are called calves.

- I make a sound like this: 'moooo'.

Everyone can have a go. If the children need prompting, prepare some questions for them, such as:

- How many legs do you have?

- What do you like eating?

- What colour are you?

- What do your babies look like?

- What sound do you make?

On the day

Unlike zoos, many farms offer opportunities for children to touch and even feed the animals. This creates excitement and stimulates discussion. The hands-on nature of the experience ensures that children will be busy and engaged throughout their visit. You can enhance their learning as the visit progresses.

Discussion

Explore the children's first impressions. Encourage them to look at and listen closely to the animals, and ask questions such as:

- What are the animals eating?

- How are they eating it?

- How are the animals moving?

- What do the animals' skins look like?

- What do the animals' skins feel like? (if the children are allowed to touch them)

Note their answers if you can, because they can be written up as labels when you return to the setting, to accompany photos that you take during the visit.

5.2 Woodmansterne Primary School's visit to Bocketts Farm

Case Study 23

Bocketts Farm, Leatherhead

Woodmansterne Primary School

Reception classes from Woodmansterne Primary School visit Bocketts Farm annually to complement their Growth and Growing topic. The school hires a coach, and ensures a ratio of one adult to five children. Parents are happy to be involved, and all accompanying adults attend a briefing session a few days before the visit. The school has drawn up a risk assessment for the visit, and it also receives the risk assessment prepared by Bocketts Farm.

The children prepare for their visit by looking at and discussing pictures of different farm animals, singing nursery rhymes such as 'Baa baa black sheep', and planting different seeds. They focus on different animals in advance on a weekly basis; for example, during Sheep Week they handle wool and discuss its origins. Just before the visit, the practitioners talk with the children about how live animals might bite or kick if agitated. This prepares the children to behave appropriately when they meet the animals.

The children always enjoy the visit. They are amazed by the size of the animals which previously they had only seen illustrated in books. The value for them lies in being able to experience at first hand the farm animals' appearances, how they smell and feel, and the noises that they make. During the visit the children are initially nervous to touch the animals but soon become more confident.

Back at the setting, the children draw their favourite animal from the farm for a display. The different experiences the children had during the visit are fed into the lesson plan for Growth and Growing, and the children's knowledge and understanding of live animals is clearly enhanced by their encounters with the animals on the farm.

Colour trail

As described on page 78, this activity encourages children to observe all the different colours they can see on the animals they encounter. The difference between this colour trail and one conducted at a zoo is that on the farm colours are likely to be more muted and less diverse. However, make sure you include orange and red for the chickens, as the feathers can sometimes be resplendent. Keep the envelopes showing the different colours of the animals, as the colour strips can be used either in a book or in a display, or as a reference for the children when they are creating any artwork as a result of the visit.

Case Study 24

Spitalfields City Farm

William Davis Primary School, London

Spitalfields City Farm is a short distance from William Davis Primary School, so the children in the nursery visit the farm at least once a term. The farm keeps cows, sheep, goats, donkeys, pigs, chickens, rabbits, guinea pigs and mice, and is supported by Sure Start Weavers and Spitalfields. Parents are encouraged to accompany their children on these visits. A translator also attends because there are many Bengali speakers in the group. The parents' involvement with these visits has led to them taking their children to the farm in their

Case Study *continued*

own time. Staff from the farm contact the setting when special events take place, and visit the setting from time to time, for example to show the children incubated eggs, using a special torch so that the chicks can be seen growing inside the shells.

The children's visit to Spitalfields City Farm complements the nursery's topics of Our Local Area, Spring (which includes Growth), and The Farm. The practitioners see significant benefits deriving from regular visits to the site. The walk to the farm motivates the children to point out features of interest, and places and people that they recognize. Once at the farm, the children react excitedly to the animals and are fascinated by their noises and movements. Some children will compare the animals to those they have seen elsewhere, such as pointing out that the cows look different from those in Bangladesh. The practitioners see new interests sparked by the visit, and have observed that some children are stimulated more effectively when learning outside the traditional nursery setting. For these children especially, the visits to the farm are particularly rewarding.

Aquariums

Aquariums can be magical places, filled with exotic creatures not usually accessible for people to view regularly or at close quarters. They offer a window to a world of communities which live in the sea, which covers over two-thirds of the planet. Aquariums often display a large range of animals, sometimes also including those which live in freshwater environments. As with zoos, aquariums communicate to visitors the global fragility of the wildlife represented at the venue, and many run conservation programmes. Some aquariums offer handling opportunities, which enable young children to learn at first hand the importance of treating living creatures with appropriate sensitivity.

Before the visit

Discussion and picture books

As with visits to zoos and farms, you can prepare the children by talking with them about the animals they will be seeing. Show the children pictures of marine life, and discuss the animals' environments. How do they compare with our own? Look through the books at your setting and pick out the ones which feature sea or freshwater creatures.

The additional activity ideas below have been reproduced with kind permission from The Deep aquarium, based in Hull.

Seaside scenario

Plan activities round a seaside theme, using stories, rhymes and the children's own experiences as stimuli. Help the children understand that the sea is home to many creatures. Look at pictures, particularly of creatures found in coastal waters.

Handling animals

If you can arrange it, study living things brought to your setting. Look for features such as shape, size, colour and body parts. Let the children get used to handling small creatures with care and concern for their welfare.

Words and movements

Discuss and act out movement words such as walk, crawl, swim, wriggle, dive, float, and sink. You can play this as the How do we move? game suggested in the Zoos section on page 76. Looking at pictures of different marine and freshwater creatures will help children think about how these animals move within the environments in which they live.

Case Study 25

Visit to The Deep, Hull

Hill House St Mary's School, Doncaster

Forty-two children from three reception classes visited the aquarium The Deep, with a ratio of one adult to every five children. The visit complemented the children's work on the topic Water. This included learning about different environments in water, habitats and life cycles of fish and amphibians. The children were also learning to swim during the term the visit was made.

The practitioner visited The Deep's website and downloaded a lesson plan for the Foundation Stage which provided ideas for preparatory activities in the setting. She also booked the children on to a workshop to take place at the venue, exploring literacy through water-related topics. For two days before the visit, the children created imaginative stories about underwater adventures.

During the visit to The Deep, the children toured the tanks and were particularly excited to encounter the sharks. The children had to behave responsibly in the darkened, quiet environment. They managed this well, and were fully occupied watching the animals around them. Their knowledge from a film about a fish provided some recognition of the wildlife they were seeing, and prompted the children to ask staff questions about the different types of creatures they were watching. This extended their development as individual learners, and improved their speaking and listening skills.

The workshop the children attended following their tour of the tanks provided hands-on, creative opportunities which explored in detail life under water. The session was based around a story about Katy the diver, who meets several different fish during her travels. This was followed up with activities enabling the children to invent new narratives and to consult fiction and non-fiction books and poetry during the process.

The ideas which had been introduced during the visit to the aquarium were developed when the children returned to the setting. The children wrote short stories about their own imaginary underwater adventures, supported by the practitioners reading to the children stories about underwater life. The children painted brightly coloured pictures of the fish they had seen during their visit, and created fish made of fabric, using a needle and thread. The setting's water tray was transformed into a sea world, with gravel providing the sea floor, weeds representing coral and toy fish as props. The children developed their language while creating new stories during their play with the water tray, and contributed new features so that it continued to develop over time.

Case Study *continued*

The visit exposed the children to new experiences and valuable encounters with animals. It was important for the children to see what an octopus looked like in reality as opposed to illustrations seen in books, and to notice an eel camouflaged against the rocks. They gained valuable information from the staff about the creatures they saw, and were interested in learning about how much bigger the sharks would grow. The children have since developed in their awareness when looking at the same species illustrated in books at the setting, and have become noticeably more interested in non-fiction books about animals. The children have also benefited from having to behave sensibly in a darkened environment and working effectively as a group.

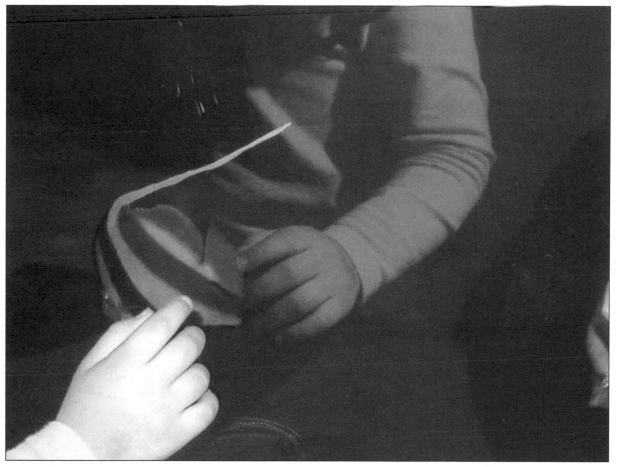

5.3 Hyde Park Barracks Nursery's visit to London Aquarium

After the visit

With some exceptions, the following suggested activities can follow any of the above visits to a zoo, farm or aquarium.

Making a book or a wall display

A way of enhancing the memories of the children's visit to the zoo, farm or aquarium is to join them in making a large book showing all that they saw on the day. You might include photos, drawings, children's comments and, if you did any of the trails described above, the colour and pattern cards at relevant points and the map showing where different sounds were heard.

These same resources could be used to create a wall display. You can add a textured effect to this by using materials representing those seen at the venue you have visited, such as wild grass or seaweed.

Looking at books

Take advantage of the recent visit by introducing the children to non-fiction books about animals. It is unlikely that the children will have seen wild animals in their natural habitat, and non-fiction books can provide background information through illustrations. They might also offer you opportunities to talk about the conservation of wildlife. You can tell the children about the dangers that animals encounter when humans hunt them or when their habitat is degraded by human activity. It's worth finding out if the zoo, farm or aquarium that you have visited runs any conservation programmes, because children's interest in this area is often raised after visits to these venues.

Small-world play

Set up a corner of your setting with small-world equipment, or provide art materials which can be used to create animals and their environments. If you don't have these, encourage the children to make their own miniature zoo, farm or aquarium, complete with the animals which are kept there. You can also include in this area books about animals, dressing-up clothes and photos taken during the visit, displayed with comments children made about the animals. These comments can be written down in the form of labels, or played as a sound installation by conducting the Animal interviews activity below.

Animal interviews

You will need:

- Sound recording equipment, for example microphone, tape recorder and cassette tape.

Encourage children to interview other children at the setting about their recent visit to the zoo, farm or aquarium. Questions can include:

- What was your favourite animal?

- What did it look like?

- What kind of noise did it make? (if the animal can make a noise)

- What other animals did you see?

- What was your favourite part of the visit?

Older children at the setting could interview the younger children, or you could be the interviewer if the children are happier answering the questions than asking them. Play the tape on a continuous loop in the corner of your setting designated for recreating the visit to the venue, so that it becomes a sound installation of the children's memories of the day.

Three-dimensional landscape

Using cardboard as a base, create a three-dimensional landscape on a clear space on the floor of your setting. Children can attach junk material like cereal boxes and yogurt pots to the base, then cover all the junk with papier-mâché mix or PVA glue mix. This surface, full of contours, bumps and dips, can then be decorated with different types of paper, material or paint. New features can be added to the landscape over time, in response to the children's play activities.

Paper plate masks

Looking at animals can inspire imaginative role-play in the setting because young children enjoy emulating their characteristics, sounds and movements. One way to encourage animal role-play is to create masks. This allows the children to transform imaginatively into animals.

To create these masks, you will need:

- Different sizes of paper plates
- Sticks for holding the paper plate mask (for example, lollypop sticks, barbecue/kebab sticks, thick twigs or dowelling rods)
- Masking tape
- Animal print tissue, paper or fur (available from educational suppliers)
- PVA glue and glue spreaders
- Wiggly eyes (optional)
- Pipe-cleaners

Children can choose the size of paper plate that best suits the animal mask they are going to create. The facial features and colours can be created using the animal print materials. Some children will cut out small patches of different print materials and stick a range of patterns on their mask, while others will choose to use only the material that corresponds to their chosen animal. It is important to allow children the freedom to create what they want and not what adults see as 'animals', even if this means a mask is produced which appears to be a combination of five different animals! Providing a range of books showing photographs of real animals can help inspire the children either way.

The wiggly eyes can add humour to the mask, but the children may want to create their own eyes out of paper or fur. (Alternatively you can cut out eye shapes if the children want to wear their masks, as opposed to holding them in front of their faces using the stick.) Pipe-cleaners can be used for whiskers as well as being bent into mouth or nose shapes. Adult assistance may be needed to staple the pipe-cleaners in place, as the glue may not hold over time. Attach the stick to the back of the plate with masking tape strips to complete the mask.

The masks can be used in a wide variety of ways, including for role-play, story-making and circle time activities. The children can give their animals names, possibly alliterated, such as Leo Lion, Catherine Cow or Zara Zebra. You could encourage the children to move around the setting in a procession – inside and outside – each child emulating their animal's movements and using their masks.

Animal bingo

This activity is appropriate following visits to zoos or farms. It requires some planning, as you will need to have a range of photographs of the animals seen at the venue. Although postcards and magazine pictures are options, photographs that the children have taken during their visit to the venue work best, as they are already familiar with them. At the setting, ask the children to make the noises of the animals and record the sounds needed for the game. An alternative is to purchase a cassette tape or CD with animal noises on it. The animal noises need to match with the photographs, and you will need several sets of photographs, depending on how many children are participating in the activity.

In a small group, share out the photographs face up and ask the children to lay their set in front of them. Play in turn the recordings of the animal noises. When the children match up a noise with a photograph, they turn that picture over. The child who matches all their photographs with the noises first is the winner.

Life-size animals

It is very exciting to make life-size models of the animals seen during your visit to the zoo, farm or aquarium. There are many ways of doing this, and they require positive adult–child interaction, always with the emphasis on the child's imagination and ideas.

Prior to making the big model, encourage the children to create large charcoal sketches of their favourite animals from the trip. (This could also be done during the visit if there is time.) These sketches can then be used as the basis for the design of the big model.

The skeleton of the animal is created using either rolled newspaper or boxes. If you are using boxes for the skeleton, let the children select from a variety of different sizes.

For a rolled newspaper animal you will need:

- Newspapers
- Masking tape
- Cellulose paste (for papier-mâché)
- Big brushes for spreading paste
- An item of furniture for the base (optional)
- Scissors
- PVA glue and glue spreaders
- Decorative materials: coloured tissue and crepe paper, fake fur, paint

You will need a large collection of newspapers to make the rolled sticks. Children and adults can make the sticks together. It is important to ensure that the sticks are fairly tight so that they are robust enough to be used to create the body shape. It is effective to use a mixture of tabloid and broadsheet newspapers, as you will then have a range of lengths.

Roll enough newspaper together to create sticks, each of about 3 cm in diameter. Wrap strips of masking tape around each stick to hold it together. If you want to make the sticks even stronger, cover them in papier-mâché paste and leave them to dry until they harden. The sticks can then be taped together to create the skeletal shape of the chosen animal. You could build your skeleton around an existing piece of furniture, such as chair or small table. This will help to make it more robust.

Once the skeletal shape is complete, you can choose to decorate it in a variety of ways using tissue paper, crepe paper or fake fur. If you use tissue paper, ensure that you apply many layers of it and cover these with diluted PVA glue, otherwise your animal will be too delicate to move around. The chosen paper could also be painted with the animal's features.

Story role-play

Create a class story in which the three-dimensional landscape, the small world animals, the masks, the animal sounds, and the large animal models from the above suggested activities are featured. You can either choose an existing storybook from your book corner which includes animals, or make up a class story inspired by the children. Children can use their masks for the characters and act out their story within or around the three-dimensional landscape. Scribe the story so that it can be copied into big print and then transferred on to card to make a big book. You could add pockets to the book within which the masks can be kept. As the book is being shared, the masks can be worn by the children to bring the story to life.

Farm shop

Children may be familiar with farmers' markets and farm shops as these are becoming increasingly popular both in rural areas and in cities. Set up a role-play farm shop with lots of different jars, boxes and tins containing pretend food. Include a cash register, food scanner and food order sheets. (You could look on the Internet to find a version of an order sheet to download and print out to use in the shop.) The children can include price lists, receipts and advertisements as part of the role-play.

Curriculum Links

1. How do we move?

2. Animal skin feely bags

3. Animal sounds

4. Colour trail

5. Pattern trail

6. Sounds trail

7. Who am I?

8. Making a book

9. Animal interviews

10. 3D landscape

11. Paper plate masks

12. Animal bingo

13. Life-size animals

14. Story role-play

15. Farm shop

Early Learning Goals	Activity	Area of Learning
Continue to be interested, excited and motivated to learn.	All	PSE: Dispositions and attitudes
Be confident to try out new activities, indicate ideas and speak in a familiar group.	1, 3, 7, 9, 14	
Maintain attention, concentrate, and sit quietly when appropriate.	6, 7	
Have a developing awareness of their own needs, views and feelings and be sensitive to the needs, views and feelings of others.	9, 14, 15	PSE: Self-confidence and self-esteem
Have a developing respect for their own cultures and beliefs and those of others.	9, 14, 15	
Form good relationships with adults and peers.	7, 9, 14	PSE: Making relationships
Work as part of a group or class, taking turns and sharing fairly, understanding that there needs to be agreed values and codes of behaviour for groups of people, including adults and children, to work together harmoniously.	2, 7, 9, 12, 14, 15	
Select and use activities and resources independently.	12, 14, 15	PSE: Self-care
Interact with others, negotiating plans and activities and taking turns in conversation.	3, 7, 9, 15	CLL: Language for communication
Enjoy listening to and using spoken and written language, and readily turn to it in their play and learning.	1, 7, 9, 14, 15	
Sustain attentive listening, responding to what they have heard by relevant comments, questions or actions.	1, 3, 6, 7, 12	
Listen with enjoyment, and respond to stories, songs and other music, rhymes and poems and make up their own stories, songs, rhymes and poems.	9, 12, 14	
Extend their vocabulary, exploring the meanings and sounds of new words.	2, 5, 7, 8, 9, 12, 14	

Early Learning Goals	Activity	Area of Learning
Speak clearly and audibly with confidence and control and show awareness of the listener, for example by their use of conventions such as greetings, 'please' and 'thank you'.	7, 9	
Use language to imagine and recreate roles and experiences.	7, 8, 9, 14, 15	CLL: Language for thinking
Use talk to organize, sequence and clarify thinking, ideas, feelings and events.	2, 7, 9, 14	
Hear and say initial and final sounds in words, and short vowel sounds within words.	8	CLL: Linking letters and sounds
Use their phonic knowledge to write simple regular words and make phonetically plausible attempts at more complex words.	8	
Explore and experiment with sounds, words and texts.	3, 8	CLL: Reading
Retell narratives in the correct sequence, drawing on language patterns of stories.	8	
Show an understanding of the elements of stories, such as main character, sequence of events, and openings, and how information can be found in non-fiction texts to answer questions about where, who, why and how.	8	
Attempt writing for different purposes, using features of different forms such as lists, stories and instructions.	8, 14, 15	CLL: Writing
Write their own names and other things such as labels and captions and begin to form simple sentences, sometimes using punctuation.	8, 14	
Say and use number names in order in familiar contexts.	7, 8	MD: Numbers as labels for counting
Use developing mathematical ideas and methods to solve practical problems.	15	
In practical activities and discussion begin to use the vocabulary involved in adding and subtracting.	7, 15	MD: Calculating
Use language such as 'greater', 'smaller', 'heavier', or 'lighter' to compare quantities.	2, 9, 10, 13	MD: Shape, space and measure
Use language such as 'circle', 'bigger' to describe the shape and size of solids and flat shapes.	2, 7, 11, 12, 13	
Use everyday words to describe position.	9, 10	
Use developing mathematical ideas and methods to solve practical problems.	15	
Investigate objects and materials by using all their senses as appropriate.	2, 6, 15	KNU: Exploration and investigation
Find out more about and identify some features of living things, objects and events they observe.	2, 6, 8, 10, 15	

Early Learning Goals	Activity	Area of Learning
Look closely at similarities, differences, patterns and change.	2, 4, 5, 6, 8, 15	
Ask questions about why things happen and how things work.	8, 15	
Build and construct with a wide range of objects, selecting appropriate resources, and adapting their work where necessary.	10, 11, 13	KNU: Designing and making skills
Select the tools and techniques they need to shape, assemble and join materials they are using.	10, 11, 13	
Find out about and identify the uses of everyday technology and use information and communication technology and programmable toys to support their learning.	8, 9, 12, 14, 15	KNU: Information and communication technology
Observe, find out about and identify features in the place they live and the natural world.	2, 6, 7, 8, 10, 12	KNU: Sense of place
Find out about their environment, and talk about those features they like and dislike.	2, 6, 8, 9, 10, 13, 15	
Move with confidence, imagination and safety.	1, 7, 14	PD: Movement
Move with control and co-ordination.	1, 14, 15	
Travel around, under, over and through balancing and climbing equipment.	1, 14	
Show awareness of space, of themselves and of others.	1, 14, 15	PD: Sense of space
Recognize the importance of keeping healthy and those things which contribute to this.	13, 14	PD: Health and bodily awareness
Recognize the change that happens to their bodies when they are active.	1	
Handle tools, objects, construction and malleable materials safely and with increasing control.	10, 11, 13 ,15	PD: Using tools and materials
Explore colour, texture, shape, form, space in two or three dimensions	2, 4, 5, 8, 10, 11, 13, 14	CD: Exploring media and materials
Recognize and explore how sounds can be changed, sing simple songs from memory, recognize repeated sounds and sound patterns and match movements to music.	6, 12, 14	CD: Music
Use their imagination in art and design, music, dance, imaginative and role play and stories.	1, 7, 10, 11, 13, 10, 14, 15	CD: Imagination
Respond in a variety of ways to what they see, hear, smell, touch and feel.	2, 4, 5, 10, 15	CD: Responding to experiences, and expressing and communicating ideas.
Express and communicate their ideas, thoughts and feelings by using a widening range of materials, suitable tools, imaginative and role-play, movement, designing and making, and a variety of songs and musical instruments.	10, 11, 13, 15	

Practical Considerations

It's easy to be discouraged from making any visits at all when faced with the lists of things which need to be done to make the experience safe and enjoyable for the children and accompanying adults. However, the more visits you make, the easier and quicker it becomes to ensure that the experience will be as free from risk as possible. Some of the tasks considered in this chapter may seem onerous to a busy practitioner, but by making that extra effort, you will enable the children to enjoy cultural riches which they may never forget and which will enhance their learning generally.

Many local education authorities (LEAs) employ an outdoor education advisor (OEA). Whatever the nature of your setting, it is recommended that you find out if your LEA has an OEA. If they do, you will save time and ease your planning by speaking with them about visits in general and about any specific visits you are planning to make. The OEA should be able to give you further information about all of the issues included in this chapter.

It is advisable to obtain appropriate public liability insurance cover, which will serve you for all your visits out of the setting. Speak to your LEA about this first, as they may provide this for you.

Roles and responsibilities

A Handbook for Group Leaders (DfES, 2002) includes a full list of responsibilities to be held by the group leader, the supervisors (accompanying adults) and the children. These are cited in the extract below, and you can access the complete handbook using the website address provided in Further Information on page 110.

Pre-visit planning

Familiarization visit

As suggested throughout this book, it is strongly recommended that you or another adult from your setting visits the venue before accompanying the children. This will help you plan the learning content, allow you to assess the space with regard to health and safety, and ease orientation on the day. There may also be an opportunity for you to discuss with staff at the venue the level of support they can provide.

From *A Handbook for Group Leaders* (DfES, 202)

(Crown copyright material is reproduced with the permission of the Controller of HMSO and the Queen's Printer for Scotland.)

Group leader

The group leader is responsible overall for the group at all times. In delegating supervisory roles to other adults in the group, it is good practice for the group leader to:

- allocate supervisory responsibility to each adult for named pupils;
- ensure that each adult knows which pupils they are responsible for;
- ensure that each pupil knows which adult is responsible for them;
- ensure that all adults understand that they are responsible to the group leader for the supervision of the pupils assigned to them;
- ensure that all adults and pupils are aware of the expected standards of behaviour.

It is good practice for each supervisor to:

- have a reasonable prior knowledge of the pupils including any special educational needs, medical needs or disabilities;
- carry a list/register of all group members;
- directly supervise the pupils (except during remote supervision) – particularly important when they are mingling with the public and may not be easily identified;
- regularly check that the entire group is present;
- have a clear plan of the activity to be undertaken and its educational objectives;
- have the means to contact the group leader/other supervisors if needing help;
- have prior knowledge of the venue – the group leader should normally have made an exploratory visit, see Standards for LEAs in Overseeing Educational Visits (see to Further Information page 110, for how to access this document);
- anticipate a potential risk by recognising a hazard, by arriving, where necessary, at the point of hazard before the pupils do, and acting promptly where necessary;
- continuously monitor the appropriateness of the activity, the physical and mental condition and abilities of the group members and the suitability of the prevailing conditions;
- be competent to exercise appropriate control of the group, and to ensure that pupils abide by the agreed standards of behaviour;
- clearly understand the emergency procedures and be able to carry them out;
- have appropriate access to first aid kits.

Each pupil should:

- know who their supervisor is at any given time and how to contact him or her;
- have been given clear, understandable and appropriate instructions;
- rarely if ever be on their own;
- alert the supervisor if someone is missing or in difficulties;
- have a meeting place to return to, or an instruction to remain where they are, if separated;
- understand and accept the expected standards of behaviour.

The designated group leader should carry out the familiarization visit. This person will have ultimate responsibility for all aspects of the visit. It is useful to select a replacement group leader in case of staff illness. This stand-in should be fully briefed about all elements of the visit in advance of the day itself.

Information for parents

Familiarizing yourself with the venue prior to your visit with the children will help you to decide the information you will need to give to parents of the children selected to go on the excursion. The information needs to show that the setting is prepared and organized, and should, ideally, include the following:

- Description of the intended visit

- Date and times

- Details of adult:child ratios

- Transport information

- Food and clothing requirements

- Permission slip

- Costs (if applicable)

Include a check-box for parents wishing to be an accompanying adult for the visit.

Design a permission slip for parents to sign at the beginning of the year which is worded so that children at your setting can be taken out at any time subject to agreed conditions. This allows you to make visits spontaneously, if necessary, lessening the administration required for each planned visit.

The children

Talking with the children about their forthcoming visit will help to build a sense of anticipation, and will highlight the learning that takes place before, during and after the event. It's also important to speak to the children about practical considerations, such as safety and behaviour. Ideas for this are given later in this chapter.

Risk assessment

A risk assessment is an essential requirement for any visit. The sample risk assessment on page 107 can serve as a template for your setting, if you have do not already have one. It is important to consider all risks, from the time the children leave the setting to when they return to it, as well as considerations for any children with special educational or medical needs. Many venues will have developed their own risk assessments of their spaces. It will save you time if you are able to obtain a copy of this before the visit.

Risk assessments should be flexible documents which can be altered in the light of the visit which has taken place.

Accompanying adults

Staffing levels in your setting are likely to lead you to seek accompanying adults from other sources, the most obvious source being parents. There is enormous value to be gained from involving the parents of children from your setting. Inviting them to share responsibility on a planned visit is an excellent way of strengthening links between them and the setting itself.

It is not a legal necessity for parents to be checked by the Criminal Records Bureau if they assist from time to time only. However, checks are obligatory if volunteers are likely to be left in sole charge of the children, or if their contact with the group is regular. Further information on how to obtain the paperwork for this can be found at http://www.disclosure.gov.uk.

The practical and learning aspects of your visit will be more successful if you convene a pre-visit meeting with all the adults who will be accompanying the children on the day. During the meeting you can brief them on the aims (including the learning aims), and talk them through the route and the planned activities. A meeting will also enable you to give them some vital health and safety information, such as that contained on the Information Card and Emergency Card (see pages 105 and 106).

It is useful to recruit at least one parent more than is necessary, in case of illness on the day.

Children with special educational needs

It is illegal to discriminate against children with special educational needs for reasons linked to their disabilities. This means that children should not be excluded from visits taking place out of the setting because of their special needs. Concerns about how such children's needs will be accommodated during the visit can be discussed in advance with their parents, the accompanying adults and a representative at the venue to be visited. Practical steps may need to be taken ahead of the visit to ensure that children with special educational needs have experiences that are as full and risk-free as those of their peers.

Numbers

Adult:child ratios

The adult:child ratios recommended by Ofsted are no fewer than one adult to every eight children over the age of 3 and no fewer than one adult to every four children aged between 2 and 3. However, many venues will have set their own rules in this area. For young children, the ratio is often one adult to every five children. Many settings prefer accompanying adults to be responsible for fewer children, for example one adult to every two or three children. This is preferable with regard to health and safety considerations, and it enhances the children's learning experience at the venue.

Clearly, small numbers of children are easier to manage than large numbers. One advantage of taking a small group is that you will need fewer accompanying adults, and are therefore more likely to recruit the required number of adult supervisors. The children are also likely to have a richer experience in a smaller group.

The most successful visits tend to involve just six to ten children at a time. If you are making visits regularly, you can rotate the children in your setting so that they all experience visits throughout the year. Some settings select participating children on the basis of their learning needs (see Case Study 26).

Case Study 26

Chelsea Open Air Nursery School

Head teacher Kathryn Solly explains how they select children to be included for each outing. The children at the Chelsea Open Air Nursery School make regular and frequent visits to cultural venues.

We generally decide as a whole staff team at a staff or planning meeting which children to select for an expedition. Each key worker has detailed knowledge of the children, their favoured learning styles, interests, needs and targets. They suggest the children whom they feel would benefit most from the stated aims of the expedition. To ensure equality of opportunity, we keep a record book to check on who goes out where and when. This book also serves as an emergency record for those out of the school, should a crisis occur. We select children either to challenge them, to provide them with opportunities for raising their self-image or to provide them with new experiences.

Length of visit

The length of your visit will depend on a number of factors, for example the nature of the venue you are visiting and where it is located. The defined length of performances will dictate how long the children stay at a performing arts venue. However, you can control the length of your visit if you are going to a museum, art gallery, local built environment, zoo, farm or aquarium. If any of these venues are offering set programmes for the Early Years, you can still decide if the children should have a chance to explore the venue in addition to participating in the programme. This decision will depend on the children's levels of concentration, and on whether the opportunities are likely to be of interest to them.

Much also depends on how regularly you make trips out of the setting, and how long it will take for you to get to the chosen destination. There will be no pressure to stay at the venue for a long time if you can make visits to it regularly. You may be happy staying for half an hour only, returning to the setting in time for lunch. If the chosen venue is further away, taking you an hour or more to reach, you may feel it a waste not to spend at least two hours at the venue, including lunch. In any case, the length of your stay at the venue should depend on the attention spans of the children. In this way, the children, not the adults, will define the nature and length of the visit.

What to take

The items listed below should equip you for most eventualities. Some of these will need to be taken by the adult leading the group; others, such as mobile phones and emergency numbers, should be held by all the accompanying adults. Emergency numbers and other essential information should be contained on an Emergency Card which can be given to all the adults involved. A sample Emergency Card is provided on page 106. A sample Information Card, which is useful for accompanying adults, is also included, on page 105.

- Mobile phone

- Emergency numbers (try to include landlines so that you don't rely solely on mobile phones)

- Spare clothes for children

- Tissues and wipes

- First aid kit

- A bottle of drinking water

- Lunch (if applicable) or snacks

- Venue details, including address and phone number

- Contact details of the adult leader of the group

Being outside/public transport

For safety reasons, the transport arrangements should be taken seriously by both the participating adults and the children. It's advisable to make sure the children know where they are going and the route they will be taking before you set out for your visit. You could act out the journey as a useful and enjoyable preparatory activity. The role-play can include being caught in a rain shower, sitting carefully on the bus or train, and holding hands with an adult at every point while on the street.

Travelling by public transport can be regarded as hazardous, but if the children know what to expect and how to behave all can go smoothly. 'Rules' can include children sitting with their backs against their seats at all times while in seated transit. Your own experience will be eased if you find out how much the fare is for each child and have the money handy to pay as soon as it is required.

At the venue

Orientation

It's easy for adults and children to feel overwhelmed when arriving at a venue for the first time. Staff at visitor attractions are aware of this, and often provide detailed instructions and maps showing which entrance needs to be used by visiting groups, and where the groups need to go once they are inside the building. You may not have this type of information if you are making a self-guided visit, but if you previously carried out a familiarization visit, you will be able to guide the group with confidence on the day. This should enhance the children's receptiveness towards new things, their learning and their enjoyment.

At large venues, it's a good idea to establish a meeting point with the other adults in your group, in case you lose contact with each other during the visit.

Lost children

Many venues will have a Lost Child policy in place, and staff will be trained in implementing it. If you lose a child in your group, you should not panic but go as quickly as possible to the reception area of the venue and report it. Venues are familiar with these situations and will often have a two-way radio system in place throughout the building or site, through which descriptions of the child will be relayed. Staff are also often trained to deal with children who have lost their adults, and will employ the building's tannoy system to alert the group's leader immediately.

You can prepare children in this important area before you set out. Assure them that it is very unlikely they will be separated from the group, but talk with them about the different things they can do if they find themselves lost. You can make labels with the name of your setting on them for the children to wear at all times during the visit (although labels are inclined to peel off). One way of helping the children to remember the name of their setting is to make up a simple song consisting of the name of your setting.

Behaviour

People of all ages need to respect the accepted codes of behaviour when visiting cultural venues. You will need to talk to the children before you visit the venue with them. How you behave depends on the nature of the site. Some pointers are given below, specific to each type of venue covered in this book. Generally, however, it's worth telling the children that everyone – adults and children – has to concentrate on their behaviour whilst in these public places. It's not something which is just required of children because they are young.

Museums and art galleries

With rare exceptions, running is not allowed in museums and art galleries. A benefit of emphasizing this to the children is that you are more likely to keep track of them while at the venue.

While shouting and screaming are never appropriate in cultural venues, talking in normal tones should be acceptable. It is generally not necessary to 'shhh' a child if they are talking. If they are referring to the works on display, it should be encouraged. However, a general consideration for other visitors in the space should be the norm.

Performing arts venues

Most performing arts venues require very different behaviour from children to what is required at museums, art galleries, zoos, farms or aquariums. Performing arts are best appreciated quietly. Some children will speak out spontaneously, often in response to the performance, and this is to be expected. However, it is useful to talk with the children in advance of the visit about behavioural expectations. Case Study 27 suggests how this might be done. Using a child's hand-print on a large sheet of paper, the five 'rules' suggested could be written and/or drawn next to each of the fingers and thumb of the print.

Case Study 27

Being an audience

Excerpt from Powys Dance activities pack for The Present

This excerpt suggests ways in which you can discuss with children beforehand the best way to behave while watching a performance. The idea comes originally from Carolyn Webster-Stratton's Dinosaur School.

Questions you can ask the children:

— Has anyone been to the theatre or seen a performance before? What happens?

— What do you do?

— How do you think we should behave when watching a performance?

Pre-visit activity:

Using the idea of a handprint, together decide on a set of 'rules' for use during the performance. Each digit can represent a different 'rule'. For example:

— Listening ears

— Watching eyes

— Quiet voices

— Still feet

— Friendly faces

The handprint can be put on display to remind children before they attend the performance.

The built environment

The behaviour of children in the outdoor urban environment has a significant impact on their safety during the visit. This needs to be clear to the children before they set out. There are some enjoyable ways you can approach this:

- Talk with the children about all the modes of transport to be found in a busy street (cars, buses, bicycles, lorries, emergency services, etc.).

- Chalk out a street scene at your setting, and take suggestions from the children as to what can be included (pavements, roads, traffic lights, pedestrian crossings, lamp posts, parking meters, etc.). Talk about how these things are useful for people walking in the street, but that sometimes there are risks involved with each of them. Discuss with the children what these might be.

■ In role-play, pretend to walk along a busy street and cross it, and talk about the importance of holding hands with a responsible adult at all times. You will find that many suggestions will be made by the children if you say, 'Watch out – something's coming our way! What is it?'

Zoos, farms and aquariums

The outdoor environment of zoos and farms can be liberating for children, but they can also present risks. It is a prime responsibility of the accompanying adults to ensure that the children in their care can be seen at all times. However, the children themselves also need to understand that they should keep their designated adult in view. Before the visit you can share a joke with the children about adults getting lost, asking the children to carefully watch out for their designated adults during their excursion.

Aquariums are usually dark, quiet places. Talk to the children before the visit about the importance of walking carefully and speaking quietly when looking at the creatures in the tanks. Respect for the animals in zoos, farms and aquariums is an important factor to communicate to the children. Discuss with them what it must be like for the animals when people disturb their environments unnecessarily.

Before the visit it is worth checking with the zoo, farm or aquarium about their own rules for children's behaviour. Some may allow running, others may not, especially indoors in such places as reptile houses or aquariums. Before your visit, talk to the children about 'inside behaviour' and 'outside behaviour', and why these might be different from each other.

A potential risk in environments with live animals is infection from E. coli 0157. The DfES advises on this fully in *A Handbook for Group Leaders*. The advice for groups visiting farms is cited in the box below. All zoos and farms have their own risk assessments addressing this area, and many provide special hand spray or cream for the children to apply before and after they pet live animals.

A Handbook for Group Leaders (DfES)

(Crown copyright material is reproduced with the permission of the Controller of HMSO and the Queen's Printer for Scotland.)

Group leaders should check the provision at the farm to ensure that:

■ eating areas are separate from those where there is any contact with animals;

■ there are adequate clean and well-maintained washing facilities;

■ there is clear information for visitors on the risks and the precautions to take.

Ensure that:

■ there is adequate trained adult supervision wherever children can come into contact with animals and need to wash their hands;

■ all children wash their hands thoroughly immediately after touching animals and before any eating or drinking;

■ shoes are cleaned and then hands are washed on leaving the farm.

Never let pupils:

- place their faces against the animals;
- put their hands in their own mouths after touching or feeding the animals;
- eat or drink while going around the farm;
- eat or drink until they have washed their hands;
- sample any animal foodstuffs;
- drink from farm taps (other than in designated public facilities);
- touch animal droppings – if they do then wash and dry hands;
- ride on tractors or other machines;
- play in the farm area, or in other areas that are out of bounds such as grain storage tanks, slurry pits, etc.

The Chief Medical Officer's revised guidance suggests:

- individual supervision by an adult for every child younger than 12 months;
- a supervision ratio of one adult for two children for children between ages one and two;
- gradually increasing ratios up to one adult for eight children for children between ages five and eight.

Financial considerations

Perhaps the biggest barrier to taking children out of the setting is cost, particularly for travel. Even if the venue you are visiting is free of charge, it is likely that you will need to arrange some transport to reach the venue – either by public transport, minibus or coach. If costs are an issue, it's always cheaper travelling by public transport, if available, than to hire a vehicle and a driver, and the practical challenges of public transport will become easier to negotiate the more you use the service.

There may be money available from external sources. Some local education authorities ensure that public transport is free to all children who are visiting venues for educational reasons. It's worth finding out what the policy is in your local authority.

Many settings have a School Fund, or ask parents to contribute to the costs of the visit. Understandably, you will wish to be discerning in your choice of venue if this fund is to be used or if you are asking parents for money. It is worth planning in advance, on a termly basis, and to know which cultural visits are likely to incur the highest costs, so you can keep these visits to a minimum. Research other venues which are either free to visit or are easy to get to on public transport, or both. These can become your more regular haunts.

Some charitable trusts may support a complete programme of cultural visits, including the cost of transport. You will need to spend time writing applications, which will need to include the aims of your proposal visits and how you will measure their success. This is an excellent way of focusing your own planning.

You can also seek to raise funds through your own initiative. Local businesses may be happy to provide what is for them a nominal sum in exchange for advertising their support to their customers. However, you should define your own policy in consultation with staff and parents before approaching commercial organizations for this kind of sponsorship.

Sample Information Card for accompanying adults

(Reproduced with kind permission from Chelsea Open Air Nursery School.)

Information for Helpers on off-site activities

1. You have been asked to support and extend the children's learning by accompanying them on a visit/expedition. This will involve you in talking to them, pointing out matters of interest and encouraging their interest and questions.

2. You will be asked to hold the hands of two children maximum. This means that you cannot push a buggy or hold the hand of a toddler.

3. Be aware of the children's safety at all times, and if in doubt check any concerns with the member of staff in charge. If anything serious happens carefully follow the instructions given by the member of staff in charge; if not, use common sense and remove yourself and the children to a place of safety as soon as possible.

4. Do ask the member of staff in charge for any detailed information you require about the visit/activity before you leave the school, as it is difficult to pay close attention to both the children in your charge and adult conversation at the same time.

5. Clearly, no helping adult should be smoking, drinking alcohol, using a mobile phone or behaving inappropriately when giving care and attention to small children.

6. A small rucksack or similar is a useful item to carry your essentials and enables you to have free hands.

7. The bottom line is – treat your charges as you would like your own children to be treated. If you have *any* worries or difficulties, consult the member of staff in charge immediately.

Sample Off-site Emergency Card for accompanying adults

(Adapted with kind permission from Chelsea Open Air Nursery School.)

IMMEDIATE ACTION CARD FOR A SERIOUS ACCIDENT OR INCIDENT

A serious accident or incident is defined as: An accident leading to a fatality, serious or multiple fractures, amputation or other serious injury; circumstances in which a party member might be at serious risk; serious illness; or any situation in which the press or media are or might be involved.

Be prepared.	Carry these instructions and the Information Card at all times.
1 First steps	Listen carefully and write down: ■ what happened; ■ to whom; ■ where; ■ when; ■ and what has happened since. Try to get a telephone number for the group and leader.
2 Next steps	Inform the Head Teacher or, if not available, a senior member of staff immediately. Setting telephone number: . . . . If you cannot make contact immediately, telephone the Local Education Authority on: . . . . Explain that it is an emergency and ask to speak to: . . . .
3 Warnings & advice	Do not speak to the press or media other than to refer them to [appropriate staff member and their contact details]. Do not let party members (staff or pupils) telephone home until contact has been made with the school or [alternative venue/agency]. Never admit liability of any sort. Do not allow anyone to see any members of the group without an independent witness being present. No one, unless they are in a relevant official capacity, has the right to see anyone who does not wish to see them. If someone tries to force a confrontation, do not do anything and call the police. Keep a written record of all that happens.

Risk Assessment Form

(Adapted with kind permission from Discover East London).

Name of setting . . . .
Venue to be visited . . . .
Date and times of visit . . . .

Date of assessment . . . .
Assessed by . . . .
Signature . . . .

Number of children . . . .
Number of adults . . . .

Potential hazard	Who might be harmed	How they might be harmed	Risk level: (High, medium or low)	How the risk can be controlled/ eliminated	Remaining risk level (high, medium or low)

Review after visit has taken place

By: . . . . Date: . . . . Points raised: . . . .

Action agreed: . . . . Deadline for action: . . . .

FURTHER INFORMATION

The following organizations, publications and websites can help you find visitor attractions and relevant resources in your local area.

Museums and art galleries

For museums and art galleries in your region:

24 Hour Museum: www.24hourmuseum.org.uk

Performing arts

Arts Council of England: www.artscouncil.org.uk/regions

Arts Council of Northern Ireland: http://www.artscouncil-ni.org

Scottish Arts Council: www.scottisharts.org.uk

Arts Council of Wales: www.artswales.org

Dance

Dance 4 – national dance agency
Tel: 0115 941 0773
www.dance4.co.uk

Music

Youth Music
A UK-wide charity set up in 1999 to provide music-making opportunities for children from 0 to 18.
Tel: 020 7902 1060
www.youthmusic.org.uk

First Notes, soundLINCS, the Lincolnshire music development agency
A music-making project established for pre-school children, their carers and pre-school practitioners.
Tel: 01522 510073
www.soundlincs.org

Drama

National Drama

The website includes resources and further information for practitioners at all curriculum levels.
www.nationaldrama.co.uk

Rogues and Vagabonds

A website devoted to theatre, including a list of children's theatre companies.
www.roguesandvagabonds.co.uk/Theatre/childrens_theatres.html

Puppetry

Puppets online

A comprehensive website listing puppet companies and puppeteers, events and information.
www.puppeteersuk.com

The built environment

CABE (Commission for Architecture and the Built Environment)

Visit this website to download a library of images which can support work on the built environment:
www.cabe.org.uk/library

Northern Architecture

Northern Architecture's education programme aims to encourage children and young people to look, question and think creatively about the built environment.
Tel: 0191 260 2191
www.northernarchitecture.com

Sightlines Initiative

The UK reference point for Reggio Children and Arts Council N.E. Early Arts Agency. *Sightlines* advocates and develops a creative approach to learning through the development of projects.
Tel: 0191 261 7666
www.sightlines-initiative.com

Zoos, farms and aquariums

Directories listing locations in the UK for these visitor attractions can be found at the following websites:

www.zoos.50megs.com
www.farmsforschools.org.uk
www.aquariauk.com

Practical considerations

A Handbook for Group Leaders, DfES
www.teachernet.gov.uk/wholeschool/healthandsafety/visits

Standards for LEAs in Overseeing Educational Visits, DfES
www.teachernet.gov.uk/wholeschool/healthandsafety/visits

Related organizations

Curiosity and Imagination (C&I)
C&I is the national organization for hands-on learning. Its website includes information about hands-on discovery centres throughout the UK.
Tel: 020 7522 6919
www.centresforcuriosity.org.uk

Stately homes

A definitive guide to stately homes in England, Scotland and Wales
www.stately-homes.com

Nature reserves and wildlife habitats

This website shows the locations of nature reserves and wildlife habitats throughout England, Scotland and Wales.
www.english-nature.org.uk

INDEX